Praise for *Perseverance and Salvation*

Three words come to mind after reading Stewart's work: simple, biblical, and practical. It is simple in the sense that he plainly and clearly treats the debated topic of salvation, particularly the issues of perseverance and faith. It is biblical because this book does not seek to defend a theological position but rather to present the full counsel of God. Finally, it is practical because the issue of salvation is of utmost importance. This is the best brief summary of this topic.

Benjamin L. Merkle
Professor of New Testament and Greek
Southeastern Baptist Theological Seminary, Wake Forest, NC

This is a delightfully accessible book concerning an issue that is crucial for every Christian. Alex Stewart presents a wonderful summary of the New Testament's teaching concerning the correlation of belief and obedience, essential to our receiving salvation in Jesus Christ promised in the gospel and assured to us by the Holy Spirit. Each chapter, brief though they are, presents vital aspects of the call of God's gospel of grace that is in Christ Jesus. Alex's chapter on gospel warnings and Spirit-given assurance of salvation effectively summarizes a core feature of *The Race Set before Us*, which I co-authored with Thomas R. Schreiner. I heartily commend Alex's book.

Ardel B. Caneday
Professor of New Testament & Greek
University of Northwestern, St. Paul

Alex Stewart has written an important book on perseverance and assurance, and he rightly shows that both themes have to be taken seriously in explaining the biblical witness. Although I would not put everything the same way Stewart does, his book should be considered by all who are attempting to understand the biblical teaching on perseverance and assurance.

Thomas R. Schreiner
James Buchanan Harrison Professor of
New Testament Interpretation
Associate Dean, The Southern Baptist Theological Seminary

Many Christians, including pastors and teachers, are not clear on the relationship between perseverance and salvation. Stewart does a fine job of bringing clarity to this issue. Readers will benefit from a coherent explanation of salvation as the Bible understands it, the necessity of perseverance for salvation, relevant texts laid out clearly, the place of assurance, and a brief but helpful discussion on the thief on the cross. Whether one has been a Christian for one year or fifty years, this book will appeal to all. One does not need to be a Seminary or Bible College student to see what Stewart so ably points out: perseverance is a major theme in the New Testament and intrinsic to salvation. Irenic and pastoral in tone, this is a must read for every Christian wanting to understand what is required to be saved.

Alan Stanley
Lecturer in Bible and Theology
Brisbane School of Theology

Alexander E. Stewart (Ph.D. Southeastern Baptist Theological Seminary) is Academic Dean and Associate Professor of New Testament Language and Literature at Tyndale Theological Seminary in Badhoevedorp, The Netherlands.

Perseverance and Salvation

What the New Testament Teaches about Faith and Works

Alexander E. Stewart

Energion Publications
Gonzalez, FL
2018

Electronic Edition ISBNs:
Kindle: 978-1-63199-507-1
iBooks: 978-1-63199-508-8
Google Play: 978-1-63199-509-5
Adobe Digital Editions: 978-1-63199-510-1

Print Edition
ISBN10: 1-63199-490-5
ISBN13: 978-1-63199-490-6

Library of Congress Control Number: 2018930819

Energion Publications
P. O. Box 841
Gonzalez, Florida 32560

energion.com
pubs@energion.com

DEDICATION

To my children: Elijah, Benjamin, Paul, Micah, Charis, and Sarah Kate. God is able to keep you from stumbling and present you blameless before his presence with great joy (Jude 24). May God begin and complete his good work in you.

TABLE OF CONTENTS

FROM THE EDITORS

The Areopagus is a hill in Athens that was once the meeting place of a Greek council. Paul preached on that hill while visiting Athens, presenting the Gospel to the Athenian council and converting one of them (Acts 17). It thus provides an excellent name for this series of booklets that examines important issues in understanding Christian beliefs and developing sound Christian practice. Each booklet is intentionally short – less than 80 pages in length – and provides an academically sound and biblically rooted examination of a particular question about doctrine or practice or an area of basic Christian belief.

The Areopagus series is orthodox in doctrine but not bound to the doctrinal statements of any denomination. It is both firm in conviction and irenic in tone. Authors have been chosen for their ability to understand a topic in depth and present it clearly.

Each book is rigorous in scholarship because we believe the church deserves no less. Yet the volumes are accessible in style as we also believe that there are many pastors and laypersons in the church who desire to think deeply and critically about the issues that confront the church today in its life and mission in the world.

In keeping with these convictions, the authors in this series are either professors who are also actively involved in ministry, pastors who have not only thought through the issues but whose ministry has been guided by their convictions, or laypersons whose faith and commitment to the lordship of Jesus Christ and his church have contributed to the Great Commission Jesus gave to all of his followers (Matt. 28:18-20).

The *Areopagus Critical Christian Issues* series is not only meant to help the church think differently. We hope that those who read its volumes will be different, for the Gospel is about the transformation of the whole person – mind, heart, and soul.

We take the words of the apostle Paul seriously when he says to the Athenians that God "has fixed a day on which he will have the world judged in righteousness by a man whom he has appointed; and of this he has given assurance to all by raising him from the dead" (Acts 17:31).

Allan R. Bevere

David Alan Black

PREFACE

This is a book about perseverance. It is not the perseverance you might associate with motivational posters of salmon
swimming up a waterfall or a mountain climber hanging from
a dangerous cliff. It is not about the power of positive thinking
to achieve difficult goals. This is about a specific kind of perseverance related to salvation and one's eternal destiny.

I am sure you know somebody who once demonstrated
faith, love, and passion for God but has since walked away from
God and is now living completely for himself or herself with no
interest in spiritual realities. Many people start well but do not
finish the race. There are three brief references to Demas in the
New Testament. Paul describes Demas as his "fellow worker"
(Philemon 24) and positively sends greetings from Demas to the
Christians in Colossae (Colossians 4:14) but later sadly notes
that "Demas, in love with this present world, has deserted me and
gone to Thessalonica" (2 Timothy 4:10; all biblical quotations
are from the ESV translation). We don't know anything about
Demas' final fate but we do know people who, in love with this
present world, have abandoned their relationship with God.

When I was a young boy (I can't remember the exact age
but it was young enough to terrify my mother) I informed my
mom that I hoped I would die as a child because I thought that
if I grew up I would abandon my faith in God and I did not want
to do that. Somehow, I had come to the conclusion that the odds
of walking away increased with age. My mother, being the good
mom that she was, quickly assured me that it would be better for
me to live and that I did not need to fear abandoning my faith
when I was older. I am very thankful for her wise counsel.

Many Christians seem to exist at one of two extremes, neither of which are biblical. Some live in constant fear that they

could lose their salvation at the drop of a hat; they are never at peace and assurance of salvation is hard to hold on to and more elusive than Bigfoot. Other Christians have an unhealthy assurance of salvation and think that because they prayed a prayer at some point in the past than it doesn't matter how they lived or what they believed in the present. They view salvation as a fire insurance policy that goes into effect and insures against potential future loss but doesn't actually have to change anything about one's day-to-day life. Neither of these extremes is healthy or correct but balance is often hard to achieve. As Christians, it is important for us to have answers to these questions:

- Can I lose my salvation?
- What happens when a Christian falls away from the faith and fails to persevere?
- How does perseverance relate to salvation?
- Is perseverance an optional extra?
- Is it automatic?

In an attempt to answer these questions this book will present an overview of the theme of perseverance in the New Testament. I am convinced the text is more important than any particular theological system and so will not be overly concerned with trying to make the texts fit a particular system, whether Calvinist or Arminian. I am guided by the conviction that even though there are diverse perspectives within the New Testament these perspectives are not contradictory. This is a massive topic and this book can do little more than present an overview in the hope of generating thoughtful reflection and discussion; it would take a series of books to exhaustively explore the many passages, questions, and rabbit trails generated by the topics of perseverance and salvation.

As you read you will notice that this book primarily focuses on passages from the New Testament and does not interact much with other books and articles. I have read and published in academic circles on these topics (see the list of recommended reading at the end), but this book is not intended to interact with other scholars but rather to guide any interested reader through the relevant and foundational New Testament passages. Since space is limited the focus of this book is exclusively on the Bible; that alone must remain the foundation for Christian thinking and beliefs. There is certainly a place for extensive footnotes and detailed interaction with other modern authors but this book is not that place. I have attempted rather to provide a clear and direct presentation of the New Testament passages that must shape our thinking about Christian perseverance. Some of the chapters below are a bit dense and you would be advised to move slowly and thoughtfully through the chapters with constant reflection on the biblical passages. This is a short book with a lot of content.

Depending upon your background, some of what I write may seem controversial. I have no desire to be controversial for the sake of controversy, but I do want to provide a challenge to some well-entrenched ideas that have only limited or partial biblical support, particularly ideas which have led to the marginalization of other biblical texts. As you evaluate what I have written let Scripture be your guide. This book is primarily aimed at Christians to help us better understand and think through our beliefs about this important topic. It assumes a basic level of understanding concerning Christianity and the Christian Gospel (good news).

My hope is that this little book on perseverance will enable you to approach the New Testament with fresh eyes in order to be transformed by God's truth. God is powerfully active in the world today to enable our faith and perseverance and I trust this book will prove to be an encouragement in this regard; an encouragement to persevere in your faith until the end no matter what the cost.

CHAPTER 1

SALVATION AND PERSEVERANCE:

CONNECTING THE DOTS BETWEEN
THE PAST AND THE FUTURE

Have you ever gotten into a disagreement with someone only later to discover that you meant different things by the words you were using? This is a particular danger in cross-cultural communication. Lawyers, politicians, and children are also quite good at exploiting the alternative meanings of words to justify behavior. "When you told me to clean my room I didn't think you meant that I needed to vacuum it."

Often people debate issues related to perseverance without meaning the same things by the words they are using. This is complicated by the fact that every Christian approaches the text of the Bible with a built-in framework (a systematic theology as it were) in place for making sense of what they read. The framework or system functions like the picture on a puzzle box (this puzzle analogy is not original with me but I cannot recall where I came across it). The illustration on the box tells you how every piece connects with every other piece to produce a clear and coherent picture. We like it when all the pieces fit together nicely; it generally makes us feel better about ourselves. Every Christian, however, faces the following challenge: How do I interpret verses that do not easily fit in my pre-understood system? This happens when a particular puzzle piece (a statement from Scripture) doesn't seem to fit the picture on the box; it looks like it should go to a different puzzle.

- Do I alter the verses to fit my system? This common option often leads to implausible interpretations of passages which do not seem to fit. It is like trimming a puzzle piece to force it to fit and hoping that nobody notices the butchered piece.
- Do I ignore the verses which don't fit? In this option we just put certain inconvenient puzzle pieces away in a drawer and subconsciously hope nobody notices they are missing.
- Do I live with some form of paradox (or negatively: cognitive dissonance)? With this option we just lay the puzzle pieces next to each other even though they don't seem to fit particularly well in the hope that as we make further progress on completing the puzzle things will work out.
- Do I alter my system to fit the verse? This is what we should be willing to do but it is actually very hard. Am I willing to admit that the picture on the puzzle box doesn't actually match the puzzle pieces I am dealing with? Fortunately, puzzle manufacturers don't do this but in my home with young children it is perfectly plausible to assume that the puzzle pieces from one puzzle may have been put into a different puzzle box. This is a particular danger with our ten different Winnie the Pooh puzzles.

The goal of this book is to keep all the pieces on the table and to allow the texts of Scripture to shape our understanding and define our terms. I would rather live with paradox than complete the puzzle by trimming the pieces or hiding some under the couch. I also believe Scripture points to a coherent picture in which all the pieces do fit; we just may have to be willing to adjust our systems and expectations of what the picture must be.

Christian perseverance is closely connected with a Christian understanding of salvation, so it is necessary to begin by looking at salvation in the New Testament.

SALVATION

An inadequate understanding of salvation is perhaps the biggest problem confronting discussions of perseverance, the New Testament warning passages, and assurance of salvation.

We generally associate salvation with the past event of conversion. Have you been saved? If you are not saved, you need to get saved. We speak of salvation as something that can be completely possessed in the present. There is, of course, biblical support for associating salvation with a past event. "For by grace you *have been saved* through faith. And this is not your own doing; it is the gift of God, not a result of works, so that no one may boast" (Ephesians 2:8–9).

Other verses that discuss salvation in terms of the beginning of the Christian life include the following:

1. "For in this hope *we were saved*" (Romans 8:24).
2. "[B]y grace you *have been saved*" (Ephesians 2:5).
3. "[God] who *saved us* and called us to a holy calling, not because of our works but because of his own purpose and grace" (2 Timothy 1:9).
4. "[H]e *saved us*, not because of works done by us in righteousness, but according to his own mercy, by the washing of regeneration and renewal of the Holy Spirit" (Titus 3:5).

These verses demonstrate that it is clearly legitimate to link salvation with conversion as a past point in time in which a believer moves from being lost to being saved.

This, however, is not the entire picture. The New Testament writers also often connect salvation with a future event which has not yet happened. We do not yet possess this future salvation. Several examples will illustrate this point. These examples are drawn from both the Greek noun (*sōtēria*) and the verb (*sōzō*) for salvation.

1. "But the one who endures to the end *will be saved*" (Matthew 10:22b).

2. "Since, therefore, we have now been justified by his blood, much more *shall we be saved* by him from the wrath of God. For if while we were enemies we were reconciled to God by the death of his Son, much more, now that we are reconciled, *shall we be saved* by his life" (Romans 5:9–10).

3. "Besides this you know the time, that the hour has come for you to wake from sleep. For *salvation is nearer to us now than when we first believed*" (Romans 13:11).

4. "If anyone's work is burned up, he will suffer loss, though he himself *will be saved*, but only as through fire" (1 Corinthians 3:15).

5. "But since we belong to the day, let us be sober, having put on the breastplate of faith and love, and for a helmet *the hope of salvation*. For God has not destined us for wrath, but to obtain salvation through our Lord Jesus Christ" (1 Thessalonians 5:8–9).

6. "Keep a close watch on yourself and on the teaching. Persist in this, for by so doing *you will save* both yourself and your hearers" (1 Timothy 4:16).

7. "Are they not all ministering spirits sent out to serve for the sake of those who *are to inherit salvation?*" (Hebrews 1:14).

8. "so Christ, having been offered once to bear the sins of many, will appear a second time, not to deal with sin but *to save those who are eagerly waiting for him*" (Hebrews 9:28).

9. "who by God's power are being guarded through faith for *a salvation ready to be revealed in the last time*" (1 Peter 1:5).

10. "Like newborn infants, long for the pure spiritual milk, that by it you may grow up *into salvation*" (1 Peter 2:2).

All of these texts describe salvation as a future event which is implicitly or explicitly tied to the return of Jesus Christ. From this perspective, believers have not yet been saved but rather have the hope of future salvation.

Is this a contradiction in the New Testament? How can I be saved and not yet saved at the same time? In light of this potential confusion most present-day Christians have focused almost exclusively on the present aspect of salvation. We generally talk about salvation in terms of Ephesians 2:8 ("you have been saved") and not in terms of Matthew 10:22 (the one who endures to the end "will be saved").

If you were to rephrase the words of Hebrews 9:28 in most churches, you would almost be looked at as an unbeliever: "I long for the day when Jesus will return to save me." Or try Romans 13:11: "Each day that passes brings me closer to the day when I will be saved." These kinds of comments may seem strange, but they fill the pages of the New Testament. The future dimension of salvation is also evident in many of the other terms we use such as "redemption," "adoption," and "justification."

1. "Now when these things begin to take place, straighten up and raise your heads, because your *redemption is drawing near*" (Luke 21:28).
2. "And not only the creation, but we ourselves, who have the firstfruits of the Spirit, groan inwardly as *we wait eagerly for adoption as sons, the redemption of our bodies*" (Romans 8:23).
3. "for by your words you *will be justified*, and by your words you will be condemned" (Matthew 12:37).
4. "For it is not the hearers of the law who are righteous before God, but the doers of the law who *will be justified*" (Romans 2:13).
5. "For through the Spirit, by faith, we ourselves eagerly wait for *the hope of righteousness*" (Galatians 5:5).

This New Testament focus on the future dimension of salvation fits very well within the Jewish context of the earliest Christians. This raises the further question: How could the earliest Christians so confidently celebrate the possession of salvation, a future reality, in the present (Ephesians 2:8–9)? If we will not be saved until Jesus returns how can we boldly proclaim that we have already been saved?

JESUS: FUTURE SALVATION BREAKS INTO THE PRESENT

Our normal focus on the present realization or possession of salvation is actually the opposite of Jewish expectations at the time of Christ. Based on Old Testament prophecies, Jews, including all of the initial Christians, expected and looked for salvation in God's future actions to rescue his people politically and economically. This confidence in future salvation was expressed in diverse hopes and expectations concerning the future day of the Lord (a day of salvation for God's people and judgment of her enemies), the coming of the kingdom of God, the pouring out of the Holy Spirit, the coming of a Messiah, a future resurrection, a future judgment, and God's renewal of creation (the new heavens and new earth described in Isaiah 65–66). These were all future hopes.

This future orientation pervades the New Testament and culminates in the visions of God's new creation in Revelation 21–22, where God acts in the future to set things right in his creation by removing sickness, death, sorrow, pain, and sin once and for all. One way this knowledge of the future impacts our present is by filling us with hope, a hope based on the firm promises of God. This hope helps to carry us through the difficulties, problems, and sicknesses that characterize our present existence.

In addition to hope, the entire New Testament celebrates the fact that God's promises about the future have already begun to be fulfilled in Jesus' life, death, and resurrection. In Christ and because of Christ's death and resurrection, future realities have been unleashed in this present evil age that is characterized by sin and death. *In Christ the future invaded the present!* Future salvation has become available in some way in the present time. This could be likened to money held in trust for a minor until the age of 21 but which began to be released early in smaller increments. This is a pervasive theme in the New Testament, but we will only focus on a few aspects of it: the kingdom of God, the Holy Spirit, resurrection, new creation, and, of course, salvation.

The Kingdom of God

When we look at the symbolic visions of Revelation 21 and 22, we are seeing the full, future realization of the kingdom of God. In that future day, God's reign and rule will be physically and tangibly present in the new heavens and earth. God will be with us and will personally wipe every tear from every eye (Revelation 21:4). The nations of the earth will exist in perfect allegiance to God (Revelation 21:24–26), and the leaves of the tree of life will bring healing to the nations (Revelation 22:2). God's reign and rule will perfectly extend through and be acknowledged by all creation. This future kingdom is spoken of throughout the New Testament (Matthew 6:10; 25:34; Luke 19:11; 21:31; Acts 14:22; 2 Thessalonians 1:5; 1 Corinthians 15:50).

In Jesus, this future kingdom invaded the present. Jesus told the Pharisees that the kingdom of God was in their midst (Luke 17:21). The kingdom was in their midst because it was embodied in the king himself. The king of God's kingdom was among them. Jesus directly linked his miracles to the coming of the kingdom: "But if it is by the finger of God that I cast out demons, then the kingdom of God has come upon you" (Luke 11:20; cf. Matthew 12:28). Even as we await the coming of God's future kingdom, we experience it to a partial degree in the present as we submit ourselves to Christ's reign, pledge and live our lives in allegiance to him, and extend his rule and presence everywhere we go. Note the present experience of the kingdom in Colossians 1:13; Revelation 1:6, 9; 5:10. Many people use the phrase "already but not yet" to describe this reality. The kingdom exists and we belong to it now (the "already), even as we wait with longing and expectation for the full realization of the kingdom in the future (the "not yet"). Paul notes that, "the kingdom of God is not a matter of eating and drinking but of righteousness and peace and joy in the Holy Spirit" (Romans 14:17). This passage clearly links our present experience of God's kingdom, reign, and rule with another future reality that has invaded the present, the Holy Spirit.

The Holy Spirit

In the Jewish thinking of Jesus' day, the outpouring of the Holy Spirit on all humanity was an event associated with the end times. This expectation was based upon Joel 2:28–29 (see also Ezekiel 36:25–27; 37:14), which stated, "And it shall come to pass afterward, that I will pour out my Spirit on all flesh; your sons and your daughters shall prophecy, your old men shall dream dreams, and your young men shall see visions. Even on the male and female servants in those days I will pour out my Spirit." Following Jesus' resurrection, the Holy Spirit was indeed poured out upon Jesus' followers as recounted in Acts 2. Peter directly interprets the outpouring of the Spirit as a fulfillment of Joel 2:28–19 in Acts 2:16.

The fruit of the Spirit is thus the fruit of the life of our future existence in God's kingdom being supernaturally produced and developed in the midst of this present evil age (Galatians 5:22–23). We are commanded to walk in the Spirit (Galatians 5:16) and the Spirit is our seal and the guarantee of our future inheritance in God's future kingdom (Ephesians 1:13–14). The outpouring of the Holy Spirit follows Jesus' resurrection, thus pointing out another feature of the future that has invaded the present: resurrection.

Resurrection

Most first century Jews, excluding the Sadducees, believed in a future resurrection that would be followed by vindication for the righteous and judgment for the wicked. Daniel 12:2 provided the background for this belief. This makes Jesus' statement to Martha particularly startling. "Jesus said to her, 'Your brother will rise again.' Martha said to him, 'I know that he will rise again in the resurrection on the last day.' Jesus said to her, 'I am the resurrection and the life. Whoever believes in me, though he die, yet shall he live, and everyone who lives and believes in me shall never die'" (John 11:23–26). Jesus was the living embodiment of the future resurrection.

Following Christ's resurrection, Paul makes it clear that those who are in Christ share in his resurrection and the power of his resurrection, even in the present! Believers are united to Christ and share in his resurrection and power over sin and death.

> For if we have been united with him in a death like his, we shall certainly be united with him in a resurrection like his. . . . Do not present your members to sin as instruments for unrighteousness, but present yourselves to God as those who have been brought from death to life, and your members to God as instruments for righteousness. . . . If the Spirit of him who raised Jesus from the dead dwells in you, he who raised Christ Jesus from the dead will also give life to your mortal bodies through his Spirit who dwells in you. (Romans 6:5, 13; 8:11)

Our present experience of resurrection power is directly linked to the Spirit who indwells us. In Ephesians 2:6, Paul describes Christians as those who have been raised up with Christ and seated with him in the heavenly places even as they continue in their present concrete, physical existence on earth (see also Colossians 3:1). Our boots are solidly on the ground in this present evil age, so to speak, but spiritually we are already experiencing the future reality of resurrection.

New Creation

Paul provides a summary description of how the future has invaded the present in 2 Corinthians 5:17. "Therefore, if anyone is in Christ, he is a new creation. The old has passed away; behold, the new has come." We normally use this verse to describe the radical and complete change that often occurs in a person's life when they turn away from their sin and turn to God in confession and faith. Perhaps you know someone who used to steal from his employer, yell at his wife and kids, and kick the dog when he was angry but after becoming a Christian experienced a total life transformation and no longer acts this way. This verse is relevant to such individual transformation, but "new creation" language was loaded language in the first century; "New creation" was not just a nice illustrative cliché pointing to a changed life.

"New creation" was a common way to point to the future world described in Revelation 21 and 22. The point of 2 Corinthians 5:17 is that in Christ this future new creation has broken into this present creation and is at work transforming those who are in Christ. Just as Jesus used the illustration of the kingdom of God being like leaven slowly spreading through an entire loaf, so new creation has broken into the present and is transforming individuals one at a time as it spreads throughout the world (Matthew 13:33).

Imagine yourself standing at the bottom of the Hoover Dam or some other immense wall holding back water. You are standing in the present, and on the other side of that wall are all of God's promises about the future. The wall is time. You can't climb over it, dig through it, or tunnel under it. There is no way you can get through the wall of time to begin experiencing the fulfillment of God's future promises about new creation. That was the experience of the Jewish people at the beginning of the first century.

Jesus' life, death, and resurrection could be thought of as the opening event, the crack in the great wall of time separating our present and God's future in the new heavens and earth. In Jesus' resurrection the future resurrection burst through the wall and opened the way for all of these other "end time" realities to come pouring out: the kingdom of God, the outpouring of the Holy Spirit, resurrection, and new creation itself. Our present experience of these future realities is as real and concrete as it is partial and incomplete, and we long for the day when Christ will return and completely remove, not just crack, the wall separating our present and God's future. The wall has cracked and life-giving water is pouring through; we are still, however waiting for the entire dam to break apart so that the whole ocean of God's future new creation could come crashing down on our heads.

Theologians have coined the phrase "inaugurated eschatology" (since theologians, of course, like big words) to describe this reality. "Inaugurated" points to the fact that these things have already begun, while "eschatology" points out the fact that the things that have already begun relate to the *eschaton* or end times. The end has begun. The end times began with the resurrection of Jesus and pouring out of the Holy Spirit. They will come to a close with the return of Christ. This perspective is pervasive in the New Testament, and the New Testament authors assume that they are living in the end times or last days (Acts 2:17; 1 Timothy 4:1; 2 Timothy 3:1, 5; James 5:3; 1 Peter 1:20; 2 Peter 3:3; 1 John 2:18; Jude 18).

Salvation

Alongside these other end-time realities, salvation has broken into the present through Jesus' death and resurrection. Salvation is first and foremost an end-time (eschatological) reality. Those who believe in Christ *will be saved* (i.e. following Christ's return they will survive the final judgment and experience eternal life in God's new creation). In the New Testament, conversion, as the initial reception of salvation, is linked with transfer into Christ's kingdom, spiritual resurrection, the reception of the Holy Spirit, and the beginning of new creation.

CONNECTING THE DOTS: PERSEVERANCE

For believers, then, salvation has two poles: a past and a future. We *have been* saved and we *will be saved*. This raises a very important question: How is the past connected to the future? How does the fact that I am saved right now in the present through faith in Jesus Christ relate to the fact that I will not be saved until he returns? Is new birth or conversion a foolproof guarantee of final salvation? Can one begin the journey of salvation and fail to finish? We will discuss these questions in the chapters ahead.

Most obviously, *the connection between the past and the future is the present.* The language of salvation is indeed used in the New Testament to describe a process of salvation in the present.

25

1. "For the word of the cross is folly to those who are perishing, but to us who *are being saved* it is the power of God" (1 Corinthians 1:18).

2. "Now I would remind you, brothers, of the gospel I preached to you, which you received, in which you stand, and by which you *are being saved*, if you hold fast to the word I preached to you—unless you believed in vain" (1 Corinthians 15:1–2).

3. "For we are the aroma of Christ to God among those who *are being saved* and among those who are perishing . . ." (2 Corinthians 2:15).

Moving beyond the specific language of salvation, I would propose that the New Testament's teaching on perseverance or endurance provides the link between the beginning of salvation and the completion of salvation, between the past and future.

"Salvation" in the New Testament is thus a very broad term that is used to describe the past, present, and future experience or reception of salvation. This understanding of salvation as past, present, and future is important for how we understand the Christian life. It also influences our understanding of assurance of salvation, the place of warnings in the New Testament, and a host of related discussions. We have been saved. We are being saved. We will be saved. Salvation is primarily a future event that we have access to in the present in Jesus Christ. We have access in the present because Jesus' resurrection punctured the wall of time separating the present and future, separating our present existence in this difficult and evil world and God's promises concerning our existence in his future new creation. We are living in a time of partial fulfillment even as we long for and wait for full-fulfillment at Jesus' return.

Hebrews 3:14 brings this together well: "For we have come to share in Christ, if indeed we hold our original confidence firm to the end." This single verse brings together conversion ("our original confidence"), final salvation ("the end"), and perseverance ("hold

. . . firm to . . ."). All three are a necessary part of coming to share in Christ.

We will cover this more in chapter five on faith and works, but it is important to note here that even though salvation covers the entire process from conversion through perseverance to final salvation, each stage in the process has the same foundation and basis. Salvation, at every point, is possible because of Jesus' death and resurrection and is experienced by grace through faith. This is important to note because it is easy for some to associate the need to persevere with some form of works-righteousness, as if perseverance were some kind of extra work needed to earn final salvation. Perseverance itself, as the day-by-day outworking of salvation in a person's life, is by grace through faith. It is not optional but neither is it some work we add on to faith in order to earn salvation. *Salvation is by grace from start to finish.*

QUESTIONS FOR PERSONAL REFLECTION OR SMALL-GROUP DISCUSSION

1. Have you ever experienced the tension noted at the beginning of this chapter between a straightforward reading of a particular verse and your understanding of what the Bible teaches? Give some examples. How do you normally respond? How have you seen others respond (adopt strained interpretations of the text, ignore verses which don't fit our pre-determined conclusions, live with paradox, change our conclusions).

2. This chapter argues that a proper understanding of salvation in the New Testament covers our entire experience and reception of God's salvation in the past (conversion), the present (perseverance), and the future (Jesus' return). Is this a new way of looking at the issue for you? At this point in the study how do you think this perspective might impact your understanding of the classic question: Can a believer lose salvation? Are there better ways to frame this popular question?

CHAPTER 2

LOOKING AT THE EVIDENCE:
PERSEVERANCE IN THE NEW TESTAMENT

In the last chapter, I suggested that perseverance or endurance should be understood as part of salvation; it is an integral part of being saved. *Perseverance is the experience and reception of salvation in the present* which connects the past event of our conversion/new birth with the future event of final salvation. Perseverance is part of the salvation which God has accomplished for us through Jesus' death and resurrection. It is not an optional extra which might be added on to salvation by super spiritual people. It is the vital connection between the past and the present. Later chapters will explore how this biblical perspective on salvation and perseverance might impact our understanding of warnings, good works, and assurance of salvation, but this chapter will provide an initial foundation for the later chapters by looking more closely at the concept of perseverance in the New Testament.

PERSEVERANCE IN THE NEW TESTAMENT

"Perseverance" and the roughly synonymous English words "endurance" or "steadfastness" are used to translate a range of Greek words in the New Testament, the most important of which are the noun *hupomonē* and the verb *hupomenō*. Other words which are less frequent but are relevant in some contexts include *makrothumia* (patience), *makrothumeō* (persevere, be patient), *hupopherō* (endure, bear up under), *stegō* (endure, put up with), *bastazō* (carry, endure), *karereō* (persevere), and *katechō* (hold fast [in some contexts]).

Throughout the remaining chapters we will examine the various "perseverance passages" found by looking at each relevant occurrence of these words in the New Testament. This approach is somewhat limited because there are many passages that touch on perseverance without using any of the actual words. For example, Revelation 2:10 states, "Be faithful unto death, and I will give you the crown of life." Likewise, Revelation 3:11 states, "Hold fast what you have, so that no one may seize your crown." Neither of these passages uses one of the Greek words for perseverance noted above, but they are both talking about perseverance.

Despite the potential drawbacks, an examination of all the passages that use the actual words for perseverance must surely form the foundation upon which further study of the theme of perseverance in the New Testament must build. This chapter will briefly present some of the general passages that discuss perseverance and later chapters will look at more controversial questions.

PERSEVERANCE AS A CHRISTIAN VIRTUE

Several passages discuss perseverance along with other Christian virtues. This is particularly common in the Pastoral Epistles.

1. "Rejoice in hope, be *patient* in tribulation, be constant in prayer" (Romans 12:12).
2. "But as for you, O man of God, flee these things. Pursue righteousness, godliness, faith, love, *steadfastness*, gentleness" (1 Timothy 6:11).
3. "You, however, have followed my teaching, my conduct, my aim in life, my faith, my patience, my *steadfastness* (2 Timothy 3:10).
4. "Older men are to be sober-minded, dignified, self-controlled, sound in faith, in love, and in *steadfastness*" (Titus 2:2).

These passages do not shed much light on the actual content of perseverance, but they do indicate that it is an important aspect of a Christian's life. More importantly, these passages "flavor" our understanding of perseverance. It is a perseverance associated with and marked by righteousness, godliness, faith, love, gentleness, patience, sober-mindedness, self-control, and prayer. Perseverance is not a virtue which has any value in isolation, as if we could stubbornly persevere in an intellectual belief in God without also persevering in righteousness, love, self-control, and prayer.

Elsewhere, Paul prays that his readers might persevere.

1. "May you be strengthened with all power, according to his glorious might, for all *endurance* and patience with joy" (Colossians 1:11).
2. "May the Lord direct your hearts to the love of God and to the *steadfastness* of Christ" (2 Thessalonians 3:5).

Paul's prayers provide a sure guide for our own prayers and in this case should lead us to pray that God would strengthen others with his power in order that they might be able to persevere with joy.

Elsewhere Paul presents himself as an example of perseverance for the churches to follow. "You, however, have followed my teaching, my conduct, my aim of life, my faith, my patience, my love, *my steadfastness*, my persecutions and sufferings that happened to me at Antioch, at Iconium, and at Lystra—which persecutions *I endured*; yet from them all the Lord rescued me. Indeed, all who desire to live a godly life in Christ Jesus will be persecuted" (2 Timothy 3:10–12). This example comes with a dismal prediction: everyone who lives godly will be persecuted. The answer to this persecution is perseverance.

Abraham, Moses, and Job are also presented as examples of perseverance.

1. "And thus Abraham, *having patiently waited*, obtained the promise" (Hebrews 6:15).
2. "By faith he [Moses] left Egypt, not being afraid of the anger of the king, for he *endured* as seeing him who is invisible" (Hebrews 11:27).

3.   "As an example of suffering and patience, brothers, take the prophets who spoke in the name of the Lord. Behold we consider those blessed who remained *steadfast*. You have heard of the *steadfastness* of Job, and you have seen the purpose of the Lord, how the Lord is compassionate and merciful" (James 5:10–11).

Abraham is presented as an example of someone who received a promise from God concerning the future, but who had to wait a long time before the reception of the promise. During this time of waiting he persevered in his faith and confidence that God would fulfill his promise, even against all odds.

Moses did not persevere on the basis of his own strength or cleverness; he did it by faith. He had a conviction of God's reality and he lived in light of that conviction. His faith is what enabled and motivated his endurance. This is important because we tend to prize human determination and success. This can trick us into thinking that perseverance is a matter of human will-power, when the reality is that human will-power is not up to the challenge. Perseverance is out of the reach of normal human ability and power; God's grace and supernatural enablement is needed and provided.

The book of Job itself is filled with references to perseverance so it was only natural that Job became a model for perseverance in Judaism and early Christianity. Those who persevere (remain steadfast) are blessed, and Job is a prime example of this reality. Job's perseverance did not earn or merit blessedness; blessedness is attributed to God's compassion and mercy.

Most important of all, Jesus himself is presented as an example for us of perseverance.

> For this is a gracious thing, when, mindful of God, one *endures* sorrows while suffering unjustly. For what credit is it if, when you sin and are beaten for it, you *endure*? But if when you do good and suffer for it you *endure*, this is a gracious thing in the sight of God. For to this you have been called, because Christ suffered for you, leaving you an example, so that you might follow in his steps. (1 Peter 2:19–21)

Jesus is the ultimate example of one who endured unjust suffering in the will of God, and we are called upon as his followers to follow in his steps of patient endurance through suffering.

The need for perseverance is often discussed in the New Testament within contexts of suffering or persecution. "Therefore we ourselves boast about you in the churches of God for your *steadfastness* and faith in all your persecutions and in the afflictions that you are *enduring*" (2 Thessalonians 1:4). "[B]ut as servants of God we commend ourselves in every way: by *great endurance*, in afflictions, hardships, calamities, beatings, imprisonments, riots, labors, sleepless nights, hunger, by purity, knowledge, patience, kindness, the Holy Spirit, genuine love" (2 Corinthians 6:4–6). Faithful perseverance is the Christian response to suffering and persecution.

PERSEVERANCE AS BEARING FRUIT, RESISTING TEMPTATION, AND WAITING WITH HOPE

Several other texts provide a general foundation for understanding what it means to persevere.

In Jesus' parable of the sower, Luke describes the seed sown in the good soil in the following way: "As for that in the good soil, they are those who, hearing the word, *hold it fast* in an honest and good heart, and bear fruit *with patience*" (Luke 8:15). Bearing fruit is often used in the New Testament as a metaphor for good works in a person's life. Jesus here indicates that one needed to receive his word and hold it fast with a good heart in order to produce fruit with perseverance.

Paul uses the language of endurance in regard to our fight against various kinds of temptation. "No temptation has overtaken you that is not common to man. God is faithful, and he will not let you be tempted beyond your ability, but with the temptation he will also provide the way of escape, that you may be able to *endure* it" (1 Corinthians 10:13). This is a powerful and precious promise. We are called upon to resist and reject temptations to sin, but we not left alone in the battle. God is faithful and will always provide the means or resources needed to endure without compromise. This links perseverance with what is commonly understood as progressive sanctification or growth in holiness, the process by which we become more like Jesus in our habits of rejecting sin and choosing what is right.

Finally, Paul uses the language of perseverance to describe our mindset and attitude as we expectantly wait for Jesus' return and the final fulfillment of all of God's promises. "But if we hope for what we do not see, we wait for it with patience [alternatively: we eagerly look forward to it with endurance]" (Romans 8:25). No generation of Christians knows if it will be the last before the second coming of Jesus but we are called upon to always live with hopeful expectation and perseverance as we wait for the fulfillment of God's promises.

CONCLUSION

This chapter has briefly surveyed a number of passages which explicitly use the Greek words for perseverance, endurance, and steadfastness, since these passages must provide the starting point for our study. Many of these passages discuss perseverance as a general Christian virtue without really commenting on what it means to persevere. Even these general passages are valuable, however, because they embed perseverance within the matrix of Christian transformation. Perseverance is our day-by-day experience of God's salvation through the ongoing work of the Holy Spirit which changes us. It changes our hearts, our desires, and our motives. Perseverance is linked closely to transformation (godliness, righteousness, love, self-control, and prayer).

Many other passages, however, link perseverance with persecution, suffering, sorrow, difficulty, and temptation. If these negative realities did not exist there would presumably be no need to persevere in faith and faithfulness. As we live in this in-between time, however, the time between the beginning and full completion of salvation, these realities do exist and perseverance is necessary.

When Jesus returns and we experience resurrection life, final salvation, in the new heavens and new earth there will be no need to persevere through suffering, sorrow, and temptation. "Now to him who is able to keep you from stumbling and to present you blameless before the presence of his glory with great joy, to the only God, our Savior, through Jesus Christ our Lord, be glory, majesty, dominion, and authority, before all time and now and forever. Amen" (Jude 24–25).

QUESTIONS FOR PERSONAL REFLECTION OR SMALL-GROUP DISCUSSION

1. Perseverance is closely connected together with righteousness, godliness, faith, love, gentleness, patience, sober-mindedness, self-control, and prayer in a matrix of Christian virtues related to transformation. Do any of these other things stand out as particularly important for perseverance? Which of these elements do you struggle with and how would a lack in any of these areas endanger our perseverance?

2. The early Christians looked to individuals in the past who persevered for encouragement and motivation: Job, Abraham, Moses, Jesus, and even Paul himself. Do such examples encourage you? What biblical or non-biblical figure has inspired you the most in your journey of faith? Why?

3. What external pressures (persecution, suffering, sorrow, difficulty, and temptation) have you experienced in your life? How have these experiences strengthened or hurt you? What have you learned from them which will impact your future perseverance?

4. Meditate for a few moments on verses 24-25 of Jude quoted at the end of the chapter. Where does this verse direct our confidence? Why is that so important?

CHAPTER 3

PERSEVERANCE:

A NECESSARY COMPONENT OR OPTIONAL EXTRA?

At the beginning of the previous chapter, I made the comment that perseverance was not an optional extra which might be added to salvation by super spiritual people. It is an essential and necessary part of salvation, a result of conversion, and the path to final and future salvation. This could be seen as a controversial claim in some circles, so it is necessary to look at the biblical evidence. This chapter will provide biblical evidence to support the claim that perseverance is necessary for final salvation. It could be said another way: no Christian will be saved without persevering until the end. Perseverance is our experience and reception of salvation in the present. It is the necessary link between the beginning of salvation in conversion and the consummation of salvation with Jesus' return in the future. This is an easy concept to grasp in almost every other area of life: it is not enough to start running a race, start writing an essay, start doing the laundry; we must actually finish! The New Testament authors likewise present perseverance as the necessary link between the beginning of salvation and the completion of salvation at the return of Jesus.

JESUS

Jesus made one particularly memorable statement about perseverance, likely uttered in at least two contexts, which seared its self on the memories of his disciples and was included in each of the first three Gospels.

1. "and you will be hated by all for my name's sake. *But the one who endures to the end will be saved.* When they persecute you in one town, flee to the next . . . ." (Matthew 10:22–23a).
2. "And because lawlessness will be increased, the love of many will grow cold. *But the one who endures to the end will be saved.* And this gospel of the kingdom will be proclaimed throughout the whole world as a testimony to all nations, and then the end will come" (Matthew 24:12–14).
3. "And you will be hated by all for my name's sake. *But the one who endures to the end will be saved*" (Mark 13:13).
4. "*By your endurance you will gain your lives*" (Luke 21:19).

The latter three references are all placed in Jesus' Olivet discourse during the final week of his life, while Matthew 10:22 occurs earlier in his ministry during the training and sending out of the twelve disciples. Each Gospel provides slightly different details but the big picture is clear. In the future there will be increasing persecution, hatred, and lack of love. In such situations perseverance will be the only response which will lead to salvation. Matthew 24:12–14 also clearly links perseverance with the proclamation of the Gospel throughout the entire world.

There is a great deal of discussion concerning the time period Jesus had in mind during the Olivet Discourse (Matthew 24; Mark 13; Luke 21). There is no doubt that some of the discourse is prophesying the destruction of Jerusalem by the Romans in A.D. 70. Each Gospel author begins the discourse with a question about the destruction of the temple and includes a prediction near the end of the discourse that all these things would take place within that generation. In addition to A.D. 70, many interpreters also think that Jesus is referring to his second coming, perhaps with the events surrounding the destruction of Jerusalem foreshadowing future events at the end of the age.

Luke's Gospel might indicate that Jesus' comment in the Olivet Discourse should be interpreted as the salvation of physical life by fleeing the city in advance of Roman armies. If this were true, Jesus' comments should not be applied to final eternal salvation at all. In response, Jesus' inclusion of the promise earlier in his ministry in his instructions to the 12 disciples in Matthew's Gospel indicates that it should not be limited completely to the historic event of A.D. 70, but rather points to a more general reality: final salvation depends upon perseverance.

PAUL

Three important perseverance passages in Paul clearly indicate the necessity of perseverance for final salvation.

1. "He will render to each one according to his works: *to those who by patience [perseverance] in well-doing seek for glory and honor and immortality, he will give eternal life*; but for those who are self-seeking and do not obey the truth, but obey unrighteousness, there will be wrath and fury" (Romans 2:6–8).

2. "*Keep a close watch* on yourself and on the teaching. *Persist in this, for by so doing you will save both yourself and your hearers*" (1 Timothy 4:16).

3. "Therefore *I endure everything for the sake of the elect, that they also may obtain the salvation that is in Christ Jesus with eternal glory.* The saying is trustworthy, for: If we have died with him, we will also live with him; *if we endure, we will also reign with him*; if we deny him, he also will deny us; if we are faithless, he remains faithful—for he cannot deny himself" (2 Timothy 2:10–13)

Romans 2:6–8 has generated a great deal of discussion, generally in an attempt to explain away what the text clearly states. We will come back to the question of good works in chapter five but for now it is enough to note that endurance in good works is integrally linked to the reception of eternal life.

First Timothy 4:16 is straightforward: Timothy needed to personally persevere and persist in his faithful teaching of the truth in order to save himself and his hearers.

Second Timothy 2:10–13 is a little more complex. Paul notes that he persevered, not for his own salvation, but for the salvation of God's elect (chosen ones). Paul then introduces a trustworthy saying about salvation and endurance, which is a bit enigmatic. On the one hand, present endurance is linked to future life in God's kingdom (reigning with him), while on the other hand Jesus will be faithful even when we are faithless. The trustworthy saying also draws a distinction between denying Christ and being faithless to Christ. Denying Jesus is much more serious than lack of faithfulness. This could support a distinction between apostasy (explicit rejection of Christ) and back-sliding.

The trustworthy saying which Paul passes along was likely developed through reflection on Jesus' words in Matthew 10:32–33. "So everyone who acknowledges me before men, I also will acknowledge before my Father who is in heaven, but whoever denies me before men, I also will deny before my Father who is in heaven."

HEBREWS

The entire book of Hebrews is an extended exhortation to persevere no matter what the cost. Every part of the book supports this purpose. The main point of the book is briefly summarized in Hebrews 10:36: "For you have need of endurance, so that when you have done the will of God you may receive what is promised." Perseverance is needed in order to receive the promise of eternal salvation.

The famous passage at the beginning of Hebrews 12 develops this point.

> Therefore, since we are surrounded by so great a cloud of witnesses, let us lay aside every weight, and sin which clings so closely, and let us run *with endurance* the race that is set before us, looking to Jesus, the founder and perfecter of our faith, who for the joy that was set before him *endured* the cross, despising the shame, and is seated at the right hand of the throne of God.

Consider him who *endured* from sinners such hostility against himself, so that you may not grow weary or fainthearted.

The "great cloud of witnesses" are the people from the Old Testament listed in the previous chapter. The faithful Old Testament believers persevered and bore witness to the fact that it was worth it! The cost was great but the reward for perseverance in faith is worth any cost. In addition to the great cloud of witnesses from the Old Testament, Jesus is presented as a model for our own endurance. He endured the shame of death on the cross and is now seated at God's right hand. We, likewise, must run with endurance the race set out for us.

REVELATION

Like the book of Hebrews, Revelation is a book about endurance. In particular, the key word in Revelation is "overcome/conquer" (*nikaō*). Each of the letters to the seven Churches in Revelation 2–3 ends with a promise of future and final salvation to the one who overcomes. "Overcoming" is presented as necessary in order to take part in God's future new creation described in Revelation 21:1–22:5. After John describes his vision of the new heavens and new earth, he notes that "The one who conquers [overcomes] will have this heritage" (Revelation 21:7a). Final salvation is limited to those who overcome. The entire book of Revelation is designed to motivate Christians to overcome no matter what the cost.

This naturally raises the question, "What does it mean to overcome?" In Revelation, many sub-themes come together to describe what it means to overcome. These themes include repentance, worship, witness, obedience, and, of course, perseverance. These five themes pervade the book of Revelation and together describe what it means to overcome. Perseverance is necessary to carry worship, witness, and obedience through time until the end, and repentance is necessary whenever we become aware of falling short in any of these areas. In five of the letters to the seven churches, this is exactly what happens. The churches are exposed for falling short and are called to repentance. The two churches, Smyrna and Philadelphia, which are not called to repentance are called to perseverance.

Several references to perseverance in the seven letters simply list it as an important Christian virtue (Revelation 2:2, 3, 19; 3:10), but other texts take it a step further and present perseverance as necessary for salvation. The church in Smyrna is told that they should expect increasing opposition and persecution which must be faithfully endured. "Do not fear what you are about to suffer. Behold, the devil is about to throw some of you into prison, that you may be tested, and for ten days you will have tribulation. *Be faithful unto death, and I will give you the crown of life*" (Revelation 2:10). Christians are instructed to face prison and death without fear because such faithfulness would lead to the crown of life, a short-hand way to describe final and eternal salvation in God's future new creation.

The promise of a crown comes up again in the letter to the church in Philadelphia: "Hold fast what you have, so that no one may seize your crown" (Revelation 3:11). Here the Christians are not called to repentance, but are instructed to persevere in their faith in order to prevent the loss of their crown.

Right at the beginning of the book, John highlights the importance of perseverance. "I, John, your brother and partner *in the tribulation and the kingdom and the patient endurance* that are in Jesus, was on the island called Patmos on account of the word of God and the testimony of Jesus" (Revelation 1:9). This verse is important because it highlights the fact that the final period of tribulation had already begun. John and his hearers were living in the tribulation right then at the end of the first century. It also indicates that John and his hearers were also participating in the kingdom in the present. Jesus was already reigning as "the ruler of kings on earth" (Revelation 1:5), and had already made Christians into "a kingdom, priests to his God and Father" (Revelation 1:6; c.f. Revelation 5:10). The kingdom and tribulation are presented as realities that were already in existence. What is necessary for John and his readers during this period of the coexistence of the kingdom with tribulation? He provides the third element: "endurance" (Revelation 1:9). Endurance enables believers to exist and thrive in God's kingdom in the present in the midst of tribulation.

Two final references to perseverance in Revelation are worth mentioning at this point (Revelation 13:10; 14:12). Often, the book of Revelation is avoided by readers because the visions are seen as difficult to interpret and understand. There are several places where John interrupts the flow of the visions to provide an interpretive comment. These comments function to apply the visions to the hearers. They are a way for John to make sure that his readers understood the main point of the visions and how they should respond to the visions.

In chapter twelve, John receives a vision of a mighty dragon, symbolizing Satan, enraged and trying to destroy Christians, "those who keep the commandments of God and hold to the testimony of Jesus" (Revelation 12:17). Chapter thirteen goes on to describe how the dragon enlists the aid of two helpers or allies in his war against Christians, two fierce beasts. The first beast is given authority to overcome and kill Christians (Revelation 13:7). The second beast carries this out by making an image of the beast, which then kills any who do not worship the image of the first beast (Revelation 13:15).

These chapters become immediately clear when we try to understand them in the way they would have been understood by the first readers. We know exactly how the first readers would have interpreted these two chapters thanks to the discovery of one letter from among a collection of letters between Pliny the Younger and the emperor Trajan from Pliny's term as governor of Pontus/Bithynia from A.D. 111–113. This is within two decades of the writing of Revelation (around A.D. 96), and within the same geographical area in which the seven churches existed (Asia Minor, modern day Turkey). The letter is also written by someone (Pliny) who had not read Revelation and did not really care anything about the early Christians. As far as historical evidence goes, this is pure gold: an independent source with no hint of literary dependence from the same geographical area within relatively the same time period!

There are many interesting details in this letter from Pliny to Trajan about Christians, but there is only space to highlight a few details here (All quotations are taken from Pliny, *Letters* 10.96–97 in the Loeb Classical Library translation by Betty Radice. I have included the full text of the relevant letters in Appendix 1). Pliny wrote to ask for Trajan's advice on the legal prosecution of Christians. He notes that some who were accused of being Christians "said that they had ceased to be Christians two or more years previously, and some of them even twenty years ago." This twenty year period is significant because it matches the writing of Revelation to within two or three years. Whatever level of persecution or social pressure which was present in Asia Minor during the time of the writing of Revelation evidently led some to abandon their faith.

Pliny explains to Trajan that if someone persistently admitted to being a Christian, "I order them to be led away for execution." On the other hand, "I considered that I should dismiss any who denied that they were or ever had been Christians when they had repeated after me a formula of invocation to the gods and had made offerings of wine and incense to your statue (which I had ordered to be brought into court for this purpose along with the images of the gods), and furthermore had reviled the name of Christ: none of which things, I understand, any genuine Christian can be induced to do."

The choice for these early Christians was quite simple and easy. If they renounced Christ and worshiped the image of the emperor and the other gods they would go free, but if they refused out of loyalty to Jesus they would be killed or tortured (as he later mentions in regard to two slave-women deaconesses). This letter from Pliny clearly anchors the visions of Revelation 12–13 in the historical situation confronting Christians in Asia Minor at the end of the first century. They could worship the image of the beast and live, or refuse to worship and be persecuted or killed. This is a choice that has explicitly confronted Christians in various places throughout history and which implicitly or subtly confronts Christians who are tempted to compromise with the beast through compromise with a culture of moral and sexual laxity.

In the middle of chapter thirteen John provides an interpretive comment to directly apply the vision of the dragon and the beasts to his first century readers (and from there to his readers throughout the centuries). "If anyone has an ear, let him hear: If anyone is to be taken captive, to captivity he goes; If anyone is to be slain with the sword, with the sword must he be slain. *Here is a call for the endurance and faith of the saints*" (Revelation 13:9–10).

The introductory phrase "if anyone has an ear, let him hear" functions to link these visions concretely back to the letters of the seven churches in Revelation 2–3 since each letter ended with the identical call to understand and respond to the message. This vision in chapter thirteen is not just applicable to believers living at the last stage of human history, but has been applicable to all Christians from the first readers until the present.

The next two lines further reinforce the earlier comment that the beast was given authority to overcome and kill Christians (Revelation 13:7). If this means that they will go into captivity or be killed with the sword because of their faithfulness to Jesus, then so be it. John concludes this interpretive interlude by directly applying the vision to his hearers: "Here is a call for the endurance and faith of the saints" (Revelation 13:10). This is the main point of application for the entire vision of the beast! So many interpreters get into such endless debates about the mark and identity of the beast that they miss the entire point of the vision. The vision is preparing God's people for the inevitability of suffering, persecution, and death before the return of Christ, and calling God's people to persevere until the end.

Although slightly less dramatically, John interrupts the visions of chapter fourteen to insert a similar comment. Right after describing the eternal punishment that awaited those who worship the beast in the present in order to avoid persecution, he notes, "Here is a call for the *endurance* of the saints, those who keep the commandments of God and their faith in Jesus" (Revelation 14:12). The reality of future judgment upon those who reject God becomes the basis to urge Christians to persevere in their obedience and faith no matter what the cost.

This discussion of Revelation is longer than our discussions of other books because perseverance as the means to overcoming and receiving final salvation is one of the main themes of the book and this theme is often ignored or missed by sensationalist claims and speculative interpretations. Revelation is incredibly relevant and applicable to the church today but not in the way that most people imagine. It is a tragedy almost beyond expression that Christians can spend hours debating how the visions in Revelation might enigmatically provide clues to present national and political events, while simultaneously missing the main point of the book, the real point of application for Christians today: we must persevere.

UNANSWERED QUESTIONS

If, as I have argued in this chapter, perseverance is necessary for final salvation, then several questions quickly follow. What does perseverance mean? What does it entail? How does one do it? Does this not make perseverance a "work" that is added on to faith? Is this just a subtle form of earning one's salvation? What about all the passages in the New Testament that speak of our assurance of salvation? If I fail to persevere do I lose my salvation? The following two chapters will explore these questions by continuing our study of New Testament perseverance passages.

QUESTIONS FOR PERSONAL REFLECTION OR SMALL-GROUP DISCUSSION

1. The main claim of this chapter is that perseverance is not an optional add-on to salvation but absolutely necessary. Do you think this claim accurately reflects the biblical passages discussed? If not, why not?

2. Have you ever considered the book of Revelation as a book primarily focused on exhorting believers to persevere? Why is this purpose often neglected in debates and discussions of the book?

3. Do you feel that the importance and role of perseverance is accurately presented to new believers? Should perseverance be included in some way in presentations of the Gospel to non-believers? Why or why not?

CHAPTER 4

PERSEVERANCE, WARNINGS, AND ASSURANCE: SECURITY IN INSECURITY?

If perseverance is necessary for salvation, then what happens to people who once appeared to have been Christians but fail to persevere? Do they lose their salvation? This is not an abstract or meaningless question. We all know people who once loved and followed God. They worshiped and served him with genuine passion, but as the years passed something changed and they are not following him today. Perhaps they are living in clear sin with no desire for repentance, or perhaps they have walked away from Christ altogether. It is at this point that our discussion of perseverance becomes very practical. Our questions about perseverance become questions loaded with eternal significance.

The questions further impact our attitude toward sin. How serious is sin in the life of a believer? At what point does "back-sliding" turn into apostasy or direct renunciation of Christ? Can a Christian who is trusting in God's grace and forgiveness choose to tolerate intentional habits of sin and still be okay? In the words of 2 Timothy 2:11–13, which we looked at in the last chapter, when does faithlessness lead into denying Christ?

The most popular way, of course, to frame these questions is to ask if Christians can lose their salvation. A very popular response, at least in North American Christianity, is "Once saved, always saved." Is this a true or accurate expression? We will come back to this expression in the conclusion of this chapter.

At the risk of engaging in dramatic over-simplification, there are two main camps that are associated with the two possible answers to the question. Painting with a broad brush, Arminians would answer that it is possible for believers to lose their salvation through apostasy (explicit denial of Christ) while Calvinists would answer that true believers (the elect) will never lose their salvation. The end result, however, is the same from either perspective. If someone abandons Christ they will not be saved whether or not they had salvation and lost it or were never saved to begin with. Because there are many differences of opinion and nuances within these broad camps, it is more helpful to avoid theological labels altogether and instead focus on the texts themselves. Those who hold that a believer can lose salvation point to the many warning passages throughout the New Testament to support their point, while those who hold that a believer cannot lose salvation point to the many assurance passages in the New Testament. Those who favor the warning passages generally minimize, ignore, or explain away the assurance passages, while those who favor the assurance passages tend to minimize, ignore, or explain away the warning passages.

It is very common for proponents of both sides to ignore, marginalize, or distort the verses that do not fit their system. I once sat through a Sunday School lesson on the warning passage of Hebrews 6 where the teacher spent the entire lesson talking about the assurance texts from other parts of the New Testament and never actually discussed the meaning or text of Hebrews 6! There are a growing number of Christians that are not content with this approach and are trying to find new ways to understand and communicate how divine sovereignty and human responsibility interact in salvation, perseverance, warnings, and assurance (see, in particular, Schreiner and Caneday, 2001). My hope is that this present book makes a contribution in this regard.

WARNING

We looked at passages in the last chapter which indicate that perseverance is necessary for final salvation. Many New Testament passages build on this reality and seek to motivate Christians to genuinely live out their faith and obedience to Jesus by warning them of the eternal consequence of not persevering. A plain and straightforward reading of these warning passages suggests 1) that they are directed toward those who appear to be genuine believers, and 2) they warn about the danger of failing to attain final salvation. Only interpretive sleight of hand can get around this plain reading of the texts. As presented in chapter one above, these warnings are all built on a broad understanding of salvation as a process through time which begins with conversion but will not reach its fulfillment until final salvation in resurrection and life in God's new creation. Salvation as a process does not mean that we add to it as we go and somehow become more saved as we add in perseverance, but rather that we experience God's salvation in Christ as individuals who are rooted in time. Salvation, as a whole, covers our experience of salvation through time from conversion, through perseverance, to final salvation. Each stage of the journey through time is described in various parts of the New Testament as salvation.

Serious warnings against falling away and not gaining final salvation fill the pages of the New Testament. Consider the following examples.

1. "So then, brothers, we are debtors, not to the flesh, to live according to the flesh. For if you live according to the flesh you will die, but if by the Spirit you put to death the deeds of the body, you will live" (Romans 8:12–13).
2. "Every athlete exercises self-control in all things. They do it to receive a perishable wreath, but we an imperishable. So I do not run aimlessly; I do not box as one beating the air. But I discipline my body and keep it under control, lest after preaching to others I myself should be disqualified" (1 Corinthians 9:25–27).
3. "Now I would remind you, brothers, of the Gospel I preached to you, which you received, in which you stand, and by which

you are being saved, if you hold fast to the word I preached to you—unless you believed in vain" (1 Corinthians 15:1–2).

4. "You are severed from Christ, you who would be justified by the law; you have fallen away from grace" (Galatians 5:2–4).

5. "Do not be deceived: God is not mocked, for whatever one sows, that will he also reap. For the one who sows to his own flesh will from the flesh reap corruption, but the one who sows to the Spirit will from the Spirit reap eternal life. And let us not grow weary of doing good, for in due season we will reap, if we do not give up" (Galatians 6:7–9).

6. "And you, who once were alienated and hostile in mind, doing evil deeds, he has now reconciled in his body of flesh by his death, in order to present you holy and blameless and above reproach before him, if indeed you continue in the faith, stable and steadfast, not shifting from the hope of the gospel that you heard, which has been proclaimed in all creation under heaven, and of which I, Paul, became a minister" (Colossians 1:21–23).

7. "Therefore we must pay much closer attention to what we have heard, lest we drift away from it. For since the message declared by angels proved to be reliable, and every transgression or disobedience received a just retribution, how shall we escape if we neglect such a great salvation?" (Hebrews 2:1–4).

8. "Take care, brothers, lest there be in any of you an evil, unbelieving heart, leading you to fall away from the living God. But exhort one another every day, as long as it is called 'today', that none of you may be hardened by the deceitfulness of sin. For we have come to share in Christ, if indeed we hold our original confidence firm to the end. . . . Therefore, while the promise of entering his rest still stands, let us fear lest any of you should seem to have failed to reach it. . . . Let us therefore strive to enter that rest, so that no one may fall by the same sort of disobedience" (Hebrews 3:12–14; 4:1, 11).

9. "For it is impossible, in the case of those who have once been enlightened, who have tasted the heavenly gift, and have

shared in the Holy Spirit, and have tasted the goodness of the word of God and the powers of the age to come, and then have fallen away, to restore them again to repentance, since they are crucifying once again the Son of God to their own harm and holding him up to contempt" (Hebrews 6:4–6).

10. "For if we go on sinning deliberately after receiving the knowledge of the truth, there no longer remains a sacrifice for sins, but a fearful expectation of judgment, and a fury of fire that will consume the adversaries. Anyone who has set aside the law of Moses dies without mercy on the evidence of two or three witnesses. How much worse punishment, do you think, will be deserved by the one who has spurned the Son of God, and has profaned the blood of the covenant by which he was sanctified, and has outraged the Spirit of grace? For we know him who said, 'Vengeance is mine; I will repay'. And again, 'The Lord will judge his people'. It is a fearful thing to fall into the hands of the living God" (Hebrews 10:26–31).

11. "See that you do not refuse him who is speaking. For if they did not escape when they refused him who warned them on earth, much less will we escape if we reject him who warns from heaven" (Hebrews 12:25).

12. "For if, after they have escaped the defilements of the world through the knowledge of our Lord and Savior Jesus Christ, they are again entangled in them and overcome, the last state has become worse for them than the first. For it would have been better for them never to have known the way of righteousness than after knowing it to turn back from the holy commandment delivered to them. What the true proverb says has happened to them: 'The dog returns to its own vomit, and the sow, after washing herself, returns to wallow in the mire'" (2 Peter 2:20–22).

13. "But I have this against you, that you have abandoned the love you had at first. Remember therefore from where you have fallen; repent, and do the works you did at first. If not, I will

come to you and remove your lampstand from its place, unless you repent" (Revelation 2:4–5).

14. "So, because you are lukewarm, and neither hot nor cold, I will spit you out of my mouth." (Revelation 3:16).

There is, of course, a wide diversity of contexts represented by these warnings, but they share several clear elements. They are all directed to Christians (or at least those who had every appearance of being Christian) and warn of a potentially real, not just hypothetical, danger. There is not space to engage in detailed comments on each text but their cumulative force is significant. *This is not a minor New Testament theme.* Perseverance is necessary, and there are strong and pervasive warnings throughout the New Testament about the dangers that accompany failure to persevere.

The function of these biblical warnings is to motivate believers to persevere and thereby be saved from God's wrath in the coming day of wrath and judgment. What happens when teachers and preachers convince people that the warnings do not apply to them? I have seen these warning passages effectively neutered time and time again as well-meaning teachers, preachers, and writers go to great lengths to try to convince their readers and hearers that these warnings somehow do not mean what they appear to mean, that somehow they mean something else, that somehow they do not apply to them.

Such neutering of these warning passages has had terrible consequences. Imagine if someone took all the warning labels off of poisonous substances and products in a store. Such an act would not automatically lead to everyone poisoning themselves (thank goodness for some level of common sense), but it would likely lead to an increased level of accidental poisonings. Similarly, even though these warning passages are not normally taught or preached with the force they have in the texts of the New Testament, most Christians maintain the idea that sin is deadly and should be avoided (thank goodness for some level of common sense). Nevertheless, well-meaning inattention or misinterpretation of these passages has led to spiritual casualties as generations of Christians have been raised with a general sense that after their conversion there is no real need for vigilance since there is no real danger. Once saved, always saved.

I use the phrase "well-meaning" because the neglect or misinterpretation of the warning passages is motivated out of a desire to be faithful to other texts of Scripture, the assurance passages. I have focused initially on the warning passages because these are the texts that I have seen neglected in my own church experience. I am fully aware that some Christian circles emphasize the warning passages to the exclusion of all else and live their lives in a constant and steady state of fear, as if they could lose their salvation at the drop of a hat. Such Christians desperately need to hear the message of the assurance passages just as I am convinced that many Christians who focus exclusively on the assurance passages desperately need to hear the message of the warning passages. We will come back to this at the end of this chapter, but first we need to look at the assurance passages that balance out the warnings. Recognition of the genuineness and seriousness of the warnings does not lead to a life of hopeless fear and insecurity.

ASSURANCE AND CONVERSION

In response to the idea that initial salvation could somehow be lost by sinful choices leading to eventual apostasy, many Christians point to the following passages which seem to tie our assurance of salvation to our conversion experience. Based on these texts, people conclude that God's promises and assurances of salvation in the present are based on conversion, the beginning of a Christian's journey.

1. "All that the Father gives me will come to me, and whoever comes to me *I will never cast out*. For I have come down from heaven, not to do my own will but the will of him who sent me. And this is the will of him who sent me, *that I should lose nothing of all that he has given me*, but raise it up on the last

day. For this is the will of my Father, that everyone who looks on the Son and believes in him should have eternal life, and I will raise him up on the last day" (John 6:37–40).

2. "My sheep hear my voice, and I know them, and they follow me. I give them eternal life, and they will never perish, and *no one will snatch them out of my hand*. My Father, who has given them to me, is greater than all, and *no one is able to snatch them out of the Father's hand*" (John 10:27–29).

3. "For those whom he foreknew he also predestined to be conformed to the image of his Son, in order that he might be the firstborn among many brothers. And those whom he predestined he also called, and those whom he called he also justified, and those whom he justified he also glorified" (Romans 8:29–30).

4. "Who shall separate us from the love of Christ? Shall tribulation, or distress, or persecution, or famine, or nakedness, or danger, or sword? . . . No, in all these things we are more than conquerors through him who loved us. For I am sure that neither death nor life, nor angels nor rulers, nor things present nor things to come, nor powers, nor height nor depth, nor anything else in all creation, *will be able to separate us from the love of God in Christ Jesus our Lord*" (Romans 35, 37–39).

5. "[He] will sustain you to the end, guiltless in the day of our Lord Jesus Christ. *God is faithful*, by whom you were called into fellowship of his Son, Jesus Christ our Lord" (1 Corinthians 1:8–9).

6. "And *I am sure of this*, that he who began a good work in you will bring it to completion at the day of Jesus Christ" (Philippians 1:6).

7. "Now may the God of peace himself sanctify you completely, and may your whole spirit and soul and body be kept blameless at the coming of our Lord Jesus Christ. *He who calls you is faithful; he will surely do it*" (1 Thessalonians 5:23–24).

The assurance represented in these texts is based on the promise of God's sovereign power at work to save his elect ("chosen people", "predestined" in the words of Romans 8:29). God is able and willing to save his people. Based upon these texts we can confidently affirm that God will save those who belong to him. This would seem to support the idea expressed above as "once saved, always saved." However, how do individuals know they are elect (are truly saved) and belong to the people of God who will surely be saved in the future day of salvation and judgment? *How does one know?*

Our confidence in God's salvation is tied to our faith throughout the New Testament. "For by grace you have been saved through faith" (Ephesians 2:8a). "[I]f you confess with your mouth that Jesus is Lord and believe in your heart that God raised him from the dead, you will be saved. For with the heart one believes and is justified, and with the mouth one confesses and is saved" (Romans 10:9–10). Salvation is inseparably linked with the presence of faith. It is those who believe God and trust in Christ alone who are saved and will be saved. From this basis, there is a level of assurance that immediately comes to a person who confesses their sin to God and trusts that he will forgive. This level of assurance is tied to conversion and new birth, to the point in time in which a person moves spiritually from being lost to being found, from death to life. Trust in God leads to complete assurance of salvation. But what about those who trust God at one point in their lives but stop trusting him at a later point?

ASSURANCE AND PERSEVERANCE

The New Testament writers were fully aware that some who started well with at least the appearance of genuine faith could back-slide, fall away, or abandon Christ in the future. We also see this reality all around us today as some who had every possible appearance of genuine salvation slide into habitual sin and eventually end up with no interest in God or salvation. What happened to the salvation of these people? How do we know that we ourselves will not, at some point in the future, follow the same course?

Above, we looked at passages that tied assurance of salvation to our confidence that God will save his chosen people, those who have believed. This is assurance tied to conversion. Many other texts in the New Testament *do not link assurance of salvation to conversion but to perseverance.* Throughout the New Testament, assurance of salvation is often based on one's works, actions, or conduct (obedience) as one lives life day by day by faith in God (1 John 2:3, 5–6, 29; 3:14, 19; 5:5–13). We are to exert effort (works) to make our calling and election sure (2 Peter 1:10–11; cf. also Galatians 5:19–23; 1 Corinthians 6:9–11; 2 Corinthians 13:5; Hebrews 6:9–12). Assurance in these texts is primarily based on the presence of the fruit of the spirit, works, sanctification, and perseverance, by which we as believers can reasonably know that we are included in God's elect and will be kept by his power. It is at this point that a closer look at some of our perseverance passages will help to clarify the discussion.

2 Peter 1:5–11

Peter exhorts his readers to "make every effort" to add various virtues or qualities to their faith. These additional qualities include virtue, knowledge, self-control, perseverance, godliness, brotherly affection, and love. Peter proceeds to note that the presence of these virtues would lead to an effective and fruitful Christian life. In contrast, "whoever lacks these qualities is so nearsighted that he is blind, having forgotten that he was cleansed from his former sins" (1:9) Peter then provides a clear and powerful statement linking perseverance and assurance: "Therefore, brothers, be all the more diligent *to make your calling and election sure*, for if you practice these qualities you will never fall. For in this way there will be richly provided for you an entrance into the eternal kingdom of our Lord and Savior Jesus Christ" (1:10–11).

Peter's readers had a level of confidence in their calling and election based upon their initial faith in Christ and conversion. Peter builds upon this by calling upon them to make their calling and election sure (*bebaian*; certain, sure, guaranteed). They are being called upon to make their salvation (calling and election) certain by adding perseverance in Christian growth to their initial saving faith. Those who do this are assured that they would never fall but would have certain access to Jesus' eternal kingdom. Assurance here is not limited to conversion, but is linked to perseverance, to continued growth in godliness, self-control, and love.

Hebrews 6:9–12

Earlier in this chapter we looked at one of the most severe warning passages in the entire New Testament, Hebrews 6:4–6. The warning itself is followed up by some very interesting comments related to assurance and perseverance:

> Though we speak in this way, yet in your case, beloved, we feel sure of better things—things that belong to salvation. For God is not unjust so as to overlook your work and the love that you have shown for his name in serving the saints, as you still do. And we desire each one of you to show the same earnestness to have the full assurance of hope until the end, so that you may not be sluggish, but imitators of those who through faith and patience inherit the promises.
> (Hebrews 6:9–12)

The warning was necessary despite the sincere hope that the readers would respond in a salvific way. Why is there such confidence that the readers would respond that way? Such a response is anticipated because of their past track record of faithfulness and service, their past work and love. Despite this confidence based upon the past, there is a continued exhortation to continue the same earnestness in the present and into the future in order to have full assurance of hope until the end. Perseverance produces full assurance of hope.

The final words exhort the readers to imitate those who through faith and patience inherited the promises. It is not a once-for-all faith linked to conversion, but a faith joined to the long passage of time with patience. It is this persevering faith which will lead to the inheritance of the promises.

James 1:2–4, 12

James begins his letter with a startlingly audacious command: "Count it all joy, my brothers, when you meet trials of various kinds, for you know that the testing of your faith produces *steadfastness* [perseverance, endurance]. And let steadfastness have its full effect, that you may be perfect and complete, lacking in nothing. . . . Blessed is the man who remains steadfast under trial, for when he has stood the test [he has been proved to have been genuine; *dokimos genomenos*] he will receive the crown of life, which God has promised to those who love him" (James 1:2–4, 12).

The description of these trials as "various" points us toward a number of possibilities including sickness, poverty, and general difficulties or sufferings, in addition to direct persecution. Why in the world would someone view suffering and difficulty as joy? James tells us that the testing of faith produces endurance, and endurance is necessary for our growth and maturity as Christians. Why is endurance necessary? Couldn't we somehow demonstrate our faith to be genuine in an easier way?

Verse twelve provides an answer by linking perseverance with final salvation. The crown of life is reserved for those who have been proved to have been genuine. The crown of life is a common metaphor in first century Judaism, the New Testament, and early Christianity for final salvation and life in God's new creation. James calls upon Christians to rejoice in trials because endurance through trials strengthens our assurance of final salvation. Endurance provides the proof that we are genuine.

Romans 5:1–11

Paul is very similar to James in his discussion of perseverance and assurance. In Romans 5:1–11, Paul discusses salvation in both the present and the future, while also discussing the link between the two. How do we know we will be saved in the final judgment? What is the basis of our assurance of salvation?

(1) Therefore, since we have been *justified* by faith, we have *peace* with God through our Lord Jesus Christ. (2) Through him we have also obtained *access* by faith into this grace in which we stand, and we *rejoice* in hope of the glory of God. (3) More than that, we rejoice in our sufferings, knowing that suffering produces endurance, (4) and endurance produces character [*dokimē*: evidence, proof that something is genuine], and character [*dokimē*] produces hope, (5) and hope does not put us to shame, because God's love has been poured into our hearts through the Holy Spirit who has been given to us.

(6) For while we were still *weak*, at the right time Christ died for the *ungodly*. (7) For one will scarcely die for a righteous person—though perhaps for a good person one would dare even to die— (8) but God shows his love for us in that while we were still *sinners*, Christ died for us. (9) Since, therefore, we have now been *justified* by his blood, much more *shall we be saved* by him from the wrath of God. (10) For if while we were *enemies* we were *reconciled* to God by the death of his Son, much more, now that we are *reconciled, shall we be saved* by his life. (11) More than that, we also rejoice in God through our Lord Jesus Christ, through whom we have now received *reconciliation*. (Romans 5:1–11)

Before initial salvation and conversion we are described as weak (5:6), ungodly (5:6), sinners (5:8), and enemies (5:10). Our present possession of salvation is described as being justified and reconciled to God. Because of Christ's death (5:9–10) and our faith (5:1), we now have been justified (5:1, 9; declared to be in the right or righteous); and reconciled to God (5:10, 11; the restoration of a broken relationship). We also now have peace with God (5:1), access to grace (5:2), and joy (5:2). This present salvation gives us confidence in future salvation. Because of our justification and reconciliation, we have confidence that we will be saved from God's wrath in the future day of judgment (5:9, 10).

How do we as believers have such incredible confidence that we will be saved on the final day of judgment? Paul here grounds our confidence in two realities. *First*, in Christ the future verdict from the final judgment has moved into the present, and right now, in the present, Christians hear the verdict of "not guilty!" This is the meaning of justification! The future verdict has been declared in the present over those whose lives are bound up with Christ's life.

Second, our faithful endurance in the midst of the suffering of this present time period produces evidence or proof (*dokimē*) that God's declaration of "not-guilty" in the present time will match his verdict in the final judgment. I think the ESV's translation of this word as "character" obscures this point (the NASB does a bit better with "proven character"). Paul's point is that we as Christians can rejoice in the midst of suffering because we know that suffering produces perseverance, and perseverance produces evidence, proof, or assurance that we are indeed in the right (justified). This assurance, forged in the furnace of endurance, then results in confident hope.

This two-fold basis of assurance guards against false assurance or false confidence. We have confidence based upon the promises of God that our faith has already resulted in justification and reconciliation. We have been saved. This confidence is confirmed or made more sure by our endurance and perseverance which results in proof or evidence that we will indeed be saved in the final judgment.

It can be charged that understanding salvation as a process experienced through time that does not culminate until the final judgment removes the importance of conversion and the associated realities of regeneration and initial justification. In response, it must be noted that conversion is still essential as the beginning of the journey, however, and not as the end. Conversion is not final salvation, but is still essential, just as the beginning of a long journey is essential to its completion. No journey will be completed unless it is first begun. Due to the assurance passages cited above it can be said with confidence in God's promises that a true beginning (conversion and new birth/regeneration) leads to the final destination (cf. Romans 8:30) by means of perseverance. It is the one who endures to the end who will be saved (Matthew 10:22; 24:13; Mark 13:13; Hebrews 10:36).

WHY THIS MATTERS

We are now at a place to provide some tentative answers to the two main questions raised at the beginning of the chapter. Can a believer lose salvation? Is "once saved always saved" a biblical expression?

Can believers lose their salvation? The question itself fails from the start because it betrays a failure to think and talk about salvation in accord with how the New Testament authors thought and talked about it. As we saw in chapter one, salvation is discussed in the New Testament with a past, present, and future. I have been saved. I am being saved. I will be saved.

If we are looking at final salvation, we cannot lose salvation because we do not yet have it. We are not there yet. The question fails because it seems to completely equate salvation with conversion-initiation; our past experience of salvation.

In contrast, many texts, particularly warning and exhortation passages, emphasize the future non-possessed aspects of salvation. The need for Christians to persevere in order to be saved in the final day motivates an obedient response to exhortations throughout the New Testament. The "not-yetness" of our salvation functions to motivate us to perseverance, while the already possessed reality of our salvation gives us assurance that we are saved by faith, and our future salvation will certainly flow from our present salvation. Our present possession of salvation gives us confidence that God has provided everything needed for our final and complete salvation

50   *Security in Insecurity*

Is "once saved always saved" a biblically accurate expression?
Again, it depends upon what one means by "saved." The expression
is almost always used with a focus on initial salvation or conversion,
the beginning of the Christian journey. In light of the warning passages noted in this chapter, it is quite difficult to defend the slogan if
the focus is on conversion-salvation. If the focus of the slogan were
to shift to final salvation it would certainly have biblical support;
i.e. once I am finally saved and living in God's new creation forever
with him I will always be saved.

In the end it does not particularly matter whether one's theology states that Christians can lose their salvation or whether those
who fall away were never genuinely saved in the first place. This
latter claim, based on 1 John 2:19, is that those who abandon the
faith were never genuinely saved. From a practical standpoint, both
positions end up at the same point. Whether you say that someone
lost their salvation or were never genuinely saved, the end reality is
the same: they are not saved now. This reality is the foundation for
the warning passages in the New Testament. Those who fail to persevere will not take part in final salvation in God's new creation. It
doesn't matter whether they lost their salvation or were never truly
saved. All that matters is that perseverance is essential in order to
bridge the gap between a conversion experience of initial salvation
and final salvation.

One could object that the way we express things does matter
because, based upon the assurance passages, God has promised to
save his elect, his chosen people. None of God's elect could possibly
fail to reach final salvation because God is the guarantee of their
salvation. This is true enough, but it misses the key point discussed
above. How does one know if he or she is elect? The New Testament
assurance and perseverance passages we discussed above will not allow us to link this knowledge exclusively to a conversion experience
of salvation in the past. We gain confidence and assurance that we
are elect in the present as we persevere in faith and faithfulness to
God. It is a living faith in God in the present which saves.

Both warning and assurance passages should be given their full weight. At various points in our lives we desperately need to hear the strong and terrifying warnings of Scripture. This is particularly the case when we are living in patterns of unconfessed and habitual sin. If I were to willingly choose to sin I ought to be afraid! This is clear from the warning against deliberate or willful sin in Hebrews 10:26. The assurance passages are not meant to provide comfort to those who are willingly and knowingly living contrary to God's will. If I use the assurance passages to comfort myself or others in the face of clear unrepentant sin, I am deceiving myself about the seriousness of sin and its consequences. The warning passages are designed to produce fear based upon the reality and danger of eternal judgment in order to motivate and move us to genuine repentance and perseverance. Healthy fear will motivate repentance.

At other points in our lives we desperately need to hear the strong and powerful assurances of God's love for us and his power to sustain us until the end and that nothing we are facing or will face is able to take us out of his hand or from his love. This is particularly important in times of weakness, sadness, depression, and despair. There is no place for us to trust our ability to persevere, as if we could accomplish it and overcome temptation and sin with just a bit more effort. Our hope is completely focused on the God who promised to save us, not only in the future, but also in the present. God's powerful promises remove fear and doubt and give us the confidence to face each day with confidence in his presence, power, and desire to carry us through this journey of life to our eternal destination with him.

My plea in this chapter is to allow the voice of both sets of texts (warnings and assurances) to be freely and powerfully heard. We desperately need the message of both. Let us stop minimizing one side in favor of the other—they are not in contradiction! The New Testament teaching on the role of perseverance in salvation unites the warning and assurance passages.

QUESTIONS FOR PERSONAL REFLECTION OR
SMALL-GROUP DISCUSSION

1. In your church community do you hear more about the warning passages or the assurance passages? What is the danger of putting too much emphasis on one set of passages or the other?

2. The warning passages are closely connected to fear. They work by reminding us to be afraid of sin and falling away. Is there such a thing as healthy fear? Why or why not?

3. 1 John 4:18 states that "perfect love casts out fear." How do you understand the relationship between God's incredible love for us and the need for healthy fear? How are the warning passages noted above related to God's love?

4. In your own experience what kind of texts do you gravitate towards and need to hear more? Warnings or assurance? Why?

CHAPTER 5

PERSEVERANCE:

HOW FAITH WORKS

If perseverance is a necessary part of salvation, does this lead to a form of works righteousness? Does it complicate and distort the simple Gospel? Does it undermine two of the great insights about salvation from the Protestant Reformation: *sola fide* (faith alone) and *sola gratia* (grace alone)? Is this legalism disguised as perseverance? Is salvation now dependent upon faith plus perseverance?

These are valid and important questions that bring us into a much larger discussion of the role of human works and activity in salvation. At the start it is important to recognize that the New Testament regularly bears witness to the necessity of works, sanctification, or perseverance in the attainment of final salvation (Matthew 25:31–46; John 8:31; 15:5–6; Romans 2:6–10; 8:12–14; 1 Corinthians 6:9–11; 9:24–27; Galatians 5:19–21; 6:7–8; Ephesians 5:5–10; Philippians 2:12–13; Col 1:21–23; 1 Thessalonians 4:1–7; 2 Thessalonians 2:13–17; Hebrews 12:14; 2 Peter 1:10–11; 1 John 1:6; 2:3, 4, 9, 15, 29; 3:1–3, 6, 7, 8, 9, 10; Jude 20–24; Rev 2:10–11). This recognition does not require a conversion to Roman Catholicism, but is rather the result of a plain and straight-forward reading of the New Testament.

The texts noted above are generally interpreted through the lens of Ephesians 2:8–9 and Romans 3:27–4:8. We are rightly convinced that salvation is clearly by grace through faith with no place for works, so whatever else these other texts about good works might mean they clearly do not mean that good works are necessary to receive God's freely offered salvation. This approach rightly prioritizes God's grace, but many Christians live with some sense of unease with the interpretation of these other passages about the apparent necessity of good works. Is there a way to faithfully bring together the biblical teaching on faith alone and grace alone with the necessity of good works and perseverance? Many interpreters take the easier road and ignore one side or the other, or avoid the issue altogether out of the fear of somehow being branded a heretic. This issue is too important for us to continue taking the easy road.

JUDGMENT ACCORDING TO WORKS

Consider the clear teaching of Scripture that the final judgment will be *in accordance with* or *on the basis of* works. This is a prominent refrain in the book of Revelation. "And all the churches will know that I am he who searches mind and heart, and I will give to each of you *according to* [*kata*] your works (Revelation 2:23; see also 18:6; 20:12, 13). Some interpreters try to make a fine nuance between judgment "according to works" and judgment "on the basis of works", but based upon the Greek this is a distinction without a difference.

According to *A Greek-English Lexicon of the New Testament and Other Early Christian Literature*, the Greek preposition *kata* idiomatically signals the "the norm according to which a judgment is rendered, or rewards or punishments are given . . . . Oft[en] the norm is at the same time the reason, so that *in accordance with* and *because of* are merged . . . Instead of 'in accordance w[ith].' κ[*ata*]. can also mean simply *because of, as a result of, on the basis of*" (BDAG *s.v.*; italics original). This observation should make an interpreter hesitant to draw fine theological distinctions based on the different English phrases "according to" and "on the basis of" in contexts of judgment, reward, and punishment.

In the book of Revelation, John makes it clear that his readers need to respond to his message with obedience and good works because the judgment of all will be based on their works. This is true of the churches (Revelation 2:23; cf. Revelation 14:13; 22:12),

Babylon (Revelation 18:6), and all of humanity (Revelation 20:12, 13). The hearers are left with no doubt that God judges all in accord with their works, and are thus motivated to respond with appropriate works (overcoming).

The conviction that God would judge all of humanity on the basis of their works was widely held and believed in both early Judaism and Christianity (see 2 Chronicles 6:23; Job 34:11; Psalm 28:4; 62:12; Proverbs 24:12; Jeremiah 17:10; Ezekiel 18:30; 24:14; 33:20; Hosea 12:2; Matthew 16:27; Romans 2:6–11; 2 Corinthians 11:15; 2 Timothy 4:14; 1 Peter 1:17). It is necessary to note that there is no negativity associated with "works" in Revelation (except, of course, evil works: Revelation 2:6, 22; 3:15; 9:20; 16:11; 18:6): good works are a necessary and important part of overcoming and persevering until final salvation (Revelation 2:2, 5; 2:19, 26; 3:2, 8; 14:13).

Many interpreters connect this judgment according to works with different levels of eternal rewards. This is certainly a possible approach to judgment according to works for Christians but it is not clearly indicated in the texts which speak about a judgment according to works.

James 2:14–26

We could look at many of the other texts listed at the beginning of this chapter but instead of a brief survey of many texts it is better at this point to look closely at one clear passage, James 2:14–26:

> (14) What good is it, my brothers, if someone says he has faith but does not have works? Can that faith save him? (15) If a brother or sister is poorly clothed and lacking in daily food, (16) and one of you says to them, "Go in peace, be warmed and filled," without giving them the things needed for the body, what good is that? (17) So also faith by itself, if it does not have works, is dead. (18) But someone will say, "You have faith and I have works." Show me your faith apart

from your works, and I will show you my faith by my works. (19) You believe that God is one; you do well. Even the demons believe—and shudder! (20) Do you want to be shown, you foolish person, that faith apart from works is useless? (21) Was not Abraham our father justified by works when he offered up his son Isaac on the altar? (22) You see that faith was active along with [*sunergeō*; working together with] his works, and faith was completed by his works; (23) and the Scripture was fulfilled that says, "Abraham believed God, and it was counted to him as righteousness"—and he was called a friend of God. (24) You see that a person is justified by works and not by faith alone. (25) And in the same way was not also Rahab the prostitute justified by works when she received the messengers and sent them out by another way? (26) For as the body apart from the spirit is dead, so also faith apart from works is dead.

A plain and straightforward reading of this text would lead to the conclusion that eternal salvation and justification are dependent on a human response of both faith and works. "Works" (doing) in James primarily indicates obedience to God and correlates to modern discussions of the process of sanctification and perseverance. The use of the word *sunergeō* (work together with) in verse 22 to describe the relationship of faith and works is particularly striking.

The Main Point

The main point of James 2:14–26 can be clearly stated: Faith without works cannot save. Positively, this point can be stated: Salvation requires both faith and works. This main point can be found by looking at 2:14d (Is such faith able to save him?), 17 (faith by itself, if it does not have works, is dead), 20 (faith without works is useless), 22 (faith was working with his works and faith was completed by works), 24 (a man is justified by works and not by faith alone), and 26b (faith without works is dead). To say that James is stressing the importance of works in a believer's life is true, but is also an understatement that falls short of his main point. The emphasis of the passage is that works are absolutely *necessary* for salvation and justification. There will be no salvation without works.

The Opening and Closing Examples: James 2:15-16, 26

The opening and closing examples used by James clearly support the main point. Both examples work by way of analogy to faith without works. The first analogy (2:15–16) answers the opening question of the section in 2:14 which reads, "What good is it . . . if someone says he has faith but does not have works? Can that faith save him?" James answers the question of 2:14 by the example of a professing believer who does nothing to help naked and starving fellow believers except to verbally encourage them. James concludes the example by asking, "What good is it?" What good has the professing believer actually done to help his naked and starving fellow believers? Absolutely nothing. James summarizes his thesis at the end of this first example by stating, "So also faith by itself, if it does not have works, is dead" (2:17). There is no benefit, advantage, or use for faith without works. It is as good as dead and can accomplish nothing.

The closing example of James 2:14–26 comes in verse 26 and makes the same point: "For as the body apart from the spirit is dead, so also faith apart from works is dead." Faith without works is analogous to a body without a spirit. Does a body without a spirit possess life? Is it useful for anything? Can it accomplish anything? Works are equated with the spirit that gives life and vitality to an otherwise dead body. The spirit/works are not just evidence or proof that life is present, *they are the life itself.* It is necessary to note that the point of the example is that both elements are required. A living person requires both a body and a spirit while salvation/justification requires both faith and works. The two examples (2:15–16, 26a), along with the parallel statements that faith without works is dead (2:17, 26b), function to bracket the discussion and clearly support the main point.

Key Words: Faith, Works, Save, and Justify

The meaning of the words "faith," "works," "save," and "jus-tify" within the book of James are the key to understanding the passage.

"Faith" is used 16 times in 12 verses in the book of James (1:3, 6; 2:1, 5, 14, 17, 18, 20, 22, 24, 26; 5:15), while the verb "believe" is used only three times in two verses (2:19, 23). James clearly views faith as positive and as absolutely necessary (1:3, 6; 2:1, 5; 5:15). James 2:14–26, however, is James' attempt to preserve a distinction between faith, joined to works, that is able to save from faith that is not able to save. Faith that is not able to save is characterized by right verbal and intellectual assent but lacks right action (2:18a, 19). Even demons possess faith that consists only of right thinking or believing (2:19). Works are what complete faith and make it salvific (2:22). They are what give life to the dead faith of verbal and intellectual assent (2:26).

"Work" is always used positively in James and occurs twice in the singular (1:4, 25) and 13 times in 10 verses in the plural (2:14, 17, 18, 20, 21, 22, 24, 25, 26; 3:13). The verb "work" occurs twice in James: once positively (1:20) and once negatively (2:9). Works are clearly defined in 3:13 as "good conduct" and are explicitly contrasted with resentful jealousy and selfish ambition (3:14). It is in James 1:19–26, however, that James clearly communicates what he means by "works" through the contrast between the hearers and the doers. This contrast in 1:19–26 illuminates James teaching in 2:14–26. The "hearers" are the ones who believe that "God is one" along with the demons (2:19), but who fail to join their faith to works for salvation as Abraham and Rahab, the "doers," did (2:21–25). James 1:19–26 describes "doing" as being slow to anger (1:19), working the righteousness of God (1:20), putting away all moral impurity and wickedness (1:21), doing the word (1:22–25), exercising self-control over speech (1:26), taking care of orphans and widows (1:27), and keeping oneself unstained from the world (1:27). Chapter two further defines "works" as showing no partiality between the rich and poor (2:1–13), and helping fellow Christians in their poverty with food and clothing (2:15–16).

It could confidently be said that James' understanding of "works" (good conduct; putting away anger, moral impurity, and wickedness; speaking rightly; keeping oneself unstained by the world) is equivalent to obedience and very close to modern conceptions of sanctification and perseverance. "Works" in James are not equivalent to Paul's discussion of "works of the law" with its focus on circumcision, food laws, etc. James nowhere indicates a focus on the ritual or ceremonial aspects of the law. The more important point to note, however, is how Paul and James conceive of works in relationship to merit. Paul is clear that any works, *whether works of the law or not,* do not earn or merit salvation (Ephesians 2:8–9). James likewise never discusses works as meritorious, but rather acknowledges that they are the result of God's will to bring forth Christians by the word of truth (1:18). Salvation is dependent on God's will (1:18), choice (2:5), mercy (2:13; 5:11), grace (4:6), compassion (5:11), and forgiveness (5:15, 20). God is therefore seen in James as the one who accomplishes salvation, and both faith and works represent the proper reception of the salvation already brought forth by God. Within this framework neither "works" nor "faith" is meritorious. Neither earns nor deserves salvation.

The verb "save" is used five times in James (1:21; 2:14; 4:12; 5:15, 20), while the noun "salvation" does not occur. The first occurrence in 1:21 follows the command to receive the implanted word which is able to save your souls. The following verses describe how one receives the word: by doing it (1:22–25). This statement that the salvation of their souls was dependent on receiving the word, further defined as doing the word, is followed in 2:14 by the question concerning whether faith without any works was able to save. James clearly answers in the negative. In 4:11–12 James is instructing believers not to judge each other because there is only one judge who is able to save and to destroy. In 5:15 it is said that the prayer of faith will save the one who is sick: the Lord will raise him up and his sins will be forgiven. The use of "save" in 5:20 is similar to 5:15 in the pairing of salvation with forgiveness of sins. The one who turns a sinner from the perversion of his way will save his soul from death and will cover a multitude of sins. The mention of final salvation in 1:21 and the connection with forgiveness of sins in 5:15 and 5:20 indicate that salvation in James cannot be limited to earthly, physical salvation or rescue, but points to the future (note the future orientation of the letter in 1:9–12, 21; 2:5; 12–13; 3:1; 4:12; 5:3, 7–9, 12).

"Justify" (declare someone righteous) is used 3 times in the book of James (2:21, 24, 25), and "righteousness" is likewise used 3 times (1:20; 2:23; 3:18). James uses "salvation" and "justification" as virtual synonyms. James begins this section by discussing whether faith without works could save. He ends the section by discussing if faith without works could justify. The change in terminology from salvation to justification is due to the introduction of Abraham as evidence and the use of "righteousness" in Genesis 15:6. Despite the change in terminology, the concept is unified throughout the section. Can faith without works save/justify someone? James' understanding of justification can therefore be seen as equivalent to Paul's: God's declaration of righteousness resulting in eternal salvation.

Making Sense of All This

James clearly indicates that faith *and* works are necessary for final, eternal salvation. "Works" in James do not indicate the ritual or ceremonial works of the law (Sabbath observance, circumcision, food laws, etc.) and they do not merit or earn salvation. Rather, works describe a life lived in obedience to God, helping others, and renouncing sin. "Works" in James point toward what some theologians call "progressive sanctification" (growth in holiness), or what we have been looking at this entire book, perseverance. Trading James' term "works" for the terms of systematic theology it could be said that James 2:14–26 is an extended argument for the *necessity* of progressive sanctification and perseverance in the attainment of final, eternal salvation/justification.

The phrase "holistic response" seems to adequately reflect this emphasis on both faith and works as the necessary human response to God's grace. Despite the fact that salvation is completely dependent on God's grace, its reception requires a holistic human response, involving the entire person (thoughts and deeds). Although many writers depict faith as the cause of works, James does not indicate a causal relationship but rather a relationship in which they are both necessary for the human reception of God's salvation. Logically faith must precede action because it is not possible to act without thinking, but James does not present faith as the cause of good works: rather he presents the necessity of both faith and works in the reception of God's salvation. To present good works as springing forth from faith is theologically and logically accurate, but it is not how James presents their relationship.

Furthermore, the emphasis in James is not on conversion, the beginning of this holistic saving response, but on perseverance, the securing of salvation in the last day by the continuation (the Greek imperfect tense of *sunergeō* in 2:22) of this holistic saving response. While James 1:18 does point to conversion and the new birth, the emphasis throughout James is the attainment of eschatological justification in the final judgment by engaging in a lifestyle of active reception of the word which is able to save (1:20). The true religion that God accepts is action (1:27).

PAUL AND JAMES IN CONTRADICTION?

Do Paul and James contradict each other on the relationship of faith and works? Compare James 2:24 and Romans 3:28.

"You see that a person is justified by works and not by faith alone" (James 2:24).

"For we hold that one is justified by faith apart from works of the law" (Romans 3:28).

It is an irony of history that the only place in the Bible where the battle-cry of the Protestant Reformation, "faith alone" (*sola fide*), explicitly occurs is James 2:24, a text which plainly says the exact opposite.

Is James right or is Paul right? Many Christians since the Protestant Reformation have clearly chosen Paul over James, but I have been arguing in this chapter that there is no reason to choose between them. They are both contained within the New Testament and neither should be used to marginalize the other. We desperately need to hear both messages. This is the diversity of Scripture whereby different authors wrote to different audiences at different times for different purposes.

James wrote to people who claimed to have faith but used their faith as an excuse for laziness and inaction. James makes the strong point that a faith that is not accompanied by a transformed life is empty and useless.

On the other hand, Paul wrote to mixed Jew/Gentile churches who were struggling with the relationship of works, particularly the works of the law, to salvation. The particular challenge in Paul's context is the claim that Jewish works of the law were required in order to be right with God and be included within the people of God. Paul strongly argues that such works are not required for justification, but that God justifies all (Jew and Gentile) on the basis of faith in Jesus Christ with no requirement of works. Paul very strongly elsewhere focuses on the necessity of good works in the life of a believer ("the obedience of faith" in Romans 1:5; 16:26; "created in Christ Jesus for good works" in Ephesians 2:10; "work out your own salvation" in Philippians 2:12).

Despite the different audiences, the reconciliation of James and Paul should not depend on the way they use the words "faith," "works," and "justify" with different meanings. Paul's argument against works cannot be limited completely to the ceremonial and ritual works of the law, and Paul and James' understanding of final justification is basically equivalent. It is true that Paul would never have conceived of saving faith as mere intellectual assent to orthodox doctrine (see the demons of James 2:19), but that point by itself does not result in reconciliation.

I propose that the key to reconciliation should rather be sought in recognition of the distinction between merit and grace. Paul's broad argument is directed against meritorious works: works engaged in to merit, deserve, or earn justification and salvation. This is what Paul seems to be opposing in Titus 3:5: "he saved us, not because of works done by us in righteousness, but according to his own *mercy*, by the washing of regeneration and renewal of the Holy Spirit, whom he poured out on us richly through Jesus Christ our Savior, so that being justified *by his grace* we might become heirs according to the hope of eternal life." Salvation is not by human achievement or righteous works. We do not and never will deserve it. It is based solely on God's mercy and grace.

James' teaching seems to make works equal in importance to faith in the reception of salvation, but denies merit to both faith and works. Salvation is God's choice and gift (James 1:18). Paul likewise often positively linked faith and non-meritorious works (Romans 1:5; 2:6–8; 6:17–18; 1 Corinthians 13:2; Galatians 5:6; 6:7–10; 1 Thessalonians 1:3). This solution seems to offer the best hope of emphasizing the unity of Paul and James without distorting the clear thrust of James' words.

Salvation by Grace
and the Necessary Human Response

It must be reiterated at this point that there is no idea present in the New Testament that faith or works earn, deserve, or merit salvation or justification. Salvation is always presented as the result of God's grace. Works are never presented as removing or covering sin; only the sacrificial death of Jesus could accomplish that. Despite the fact that salvation is completely dependent on God's grace, it requires a human response. The connection between God's grace and our human response is clearly presented in James 1:18–20. God gives birth to individuals by the word of truth (1:18), yet

James also urges his hearers to receive the implanted word which was able to save their souls (1:21). God gives salvation freely and we are called upon to receive it.

The necessary human response is often wrongly presented as simple faith (often implicitly understood as intellectual assent to a list of facts about God) in contrast to any works, as if correct, saving thinking could exist independently of right acting. This false dichotomy cannot stand in light of the evidence of the New Testament documents themselves (see the texts listed at the beginning of this chapter). There can be no compartmentalization. A saving human response to God's initiative of grace is consistently understood as holistic, involving the entire person. This holistic response involves a person responding to and receiving God's grace as a whole person, with a subsequent impact on every area of life (thought, word, and action). If a person's life is not changed on the level of actions they will not be saved because actions and faith are inseparably connected to each other and to God's transformative work of salvation. A holistic response of faith involves a radical reorientation of a person's entire being.

I could tell you all day long that I believe stealing is wrong but if I repeatedly shoplift from stores, what do I truly believe about stealing? Despite what I might claim to believe about stealing my actions will reflect what I truly believe. We are fooling ourselves when we try to convince ourselves that our actions are somehow disconnected from what we claim to believe. "Faith" and "belief" are ambiguous words that could range from a mere opinion to a life changing and behavior transforming conviction. Holistic saving faith in the New Testament is the latter; it is not on the level of opinion but on the level of life transformation and reorientation. This is why repentance is so central in the proclamation of the Gospel (Acts 2:38; note how faith is implicitly but not explicitly included in Peter's instructions).

We have seen throughout this book that "salvation" in the New Testament is used to describe our experience of salvation in the past, the present, and the future. Salvation is simultaneously "already" but "not yet" possessed by Christians. Despite the fact that this "already" but "not yet" dimension of salvation is well known, its significance for understanding the New Testament's teaching on faith, works, assurance, warning, and salvation is often neglected. As we saw in the last chapter, the assurance passages are generally based on the "already" possessed aspect of our salvation, while the warning passages are tied to the fact that salvation is not yet fully consummated, it is "not yet" possessed.

Despite this New Testament perspective, salvation is almost always spoken of by modern Christians in the past tense, and the need to be saved is directed solely to unbelievers. The New Testament evidence more often than not speaks of salvation as a future event and confronts Christians with the continuing need to be saved. Faith and works are the necessary, persevering, holistic, receptive human response at every point in this process of salvation from its inception to its culmination in resurrection life in God's new creation.

WHAT ABOUT . . . ?

Before concluding, a brief response can be offered to an obvious objection: this understanding of the holistic necessity of faith *and* works understood as sanctification and perseverance is synergistic: i.e. works-based. In response both "yes" and "no" can be said. As noted above, James uses the verb *sunergeō* (work together with; James 2:22) to describe his holistic understanding of the relationship between faith and works as the required human response to God's grace. Since the Reformation, the idea of faith and works working together for salvation has acquired entirely negative connotations in light of Paul's polemical battle against works-based righteousness. It would be naïve to think that "synergism" could ever be positively rehabilitated in the modern church in light of James' usage, but the truth communicated by the word in James must regain its place in Christian thinking. Therefore, according to James' usage of the term in James 2:22, this study does support the synergism of faith and works for salvation if the synergism is understood as a holistic receptive response of a person to God's freely offered salvation.

On the other hand, as defined by Paul's polemical battle against works righteousness, it certainly is not synergistic (Ephesians 2:8–10). According to James 2:22, there is a synergism of faith and works in our human response but there is not a synergism of God's efforts and the efforts of humans to achieve salvation. Salvation is based on God's grace from beginning to end. Faith, works, sanctification and perseverance cannot earn or merit salvation, and are all results of God's active, saving grace. They are, however, all necessary dimensions of a holistic human response of reception and thanksgiving to the salvation freely offered by God on the basis of the work of Christ on the cross. Christ's atonement is what saves people. Genuine faith expressed in repentance and works of obedience is the necessary human response; it is the way that we receive God's gift.

The example of the thief on the cross (Luke 23:39–43) does not invalidate the idea that perseverance is necessary for salvation because it introduces the misleading question of "how much work is enough?" To think of works, sanctification, or perseverance in terms of "how much" is to wrongly view biblical works as meritorious. The question should rather be whether or not the thief responded holistically in such a way that his entire being (thought and action) was committed to Christ. From his verbal response to the other thief (Luke 23:40–41) one can reasonably deduce that he did holistically respond in faith to Jesus and, if he had lived, his life surely would have reflected faith *and* works of obedience to Christ. Perseverance is the biblical response to merit-driven perfectionism. We will never be perfect until Jesus returns, but we must persevere in genuine, works-producing faith.

PULLING THINGS TOGETHER

"Works" in the book of James can be equated to modern theological discussions of sanctification or perseverance. Works are essential and necessary for salvation, not simply as evidence or proof of an inward change, but as part of the holistic response of an individual to God's grace. Such a holistic response will affect all of a person's life: ones' thoughts and actions. Such a holistic response to God's initiative of grace in Christ will result in final salvation through its perseverance to the end.

This understanding of the teaching of James 2:14–26 in relationship to the rest of the New Testament does not allow for us to focus exclusively on the past event of conversion/salvation, but rather views salvation as a temporal progression that begins with conversion and awaits its ultimate fulfillment and vindication in the return of Christ and God's new creation. This understanding also gives appropriate weight to biblical warnings and promises of assurance and is the biblical remedy for easy-believism, dead orthodoxy, and cheap grace.

Faith and works do not merit or earn salvation but are the appropriate and necessary human response to God's gracious offer of salvation because they engage us at every level of our being, our thoughts and choices. A sharp dichotomy between faith and works fails to comprehend their interconnectedness. A person will not act a certain way without belief that this is how they should act. Conversely, a person's actions clearly demonstrate what they truly believe. We must forever reject the notion that saving faith is an intellectual commitment that can somehow exist and be effective as a disembodied belief with no concrete connection to the real world. As James argues, works give life to the dead and useless body of faith alone (James 2:26).

QUESTIONS FOR PERSONAL REFLECTION OR
SMALL-GROUP DISCUSSION

1. How has this chapter challenged you to reconsider your understanding of the relationship between faith and works?

2. Do you agree that saving faith must go beyond mere intellectual assent to a list of facts about God? Why or why not?

3. Does it make sense to you to think of saving faith as a reorientation of the direction of someone's entire life? Does this understanding of saving faith work to bring together the biblical teaching on faith and works? Why or why not?

CHAPTER 6

THE SECRET INGREDIENT

I have sought in this book to highlight New Testament passages which are regularly minimized, distorted, or explained away by interpretive magic tricks or sleight of hand. Some Christians regularly ignore the warning passages in favor of the assurance passages, while others stress the warning passages to such an extent that there is little place left for assurance. Some Christians regularly ignore the New Testament teaching about the necessity of perseverance in good works in favor of passages that stress faith while others stress the passages on good works and ignore the passages about faith. As noted in chapter one, such approaches to the New Testament resemble a person trying to put a puzzle together while simultaneously throwing away the pieces that do not initially seem to fit. I hope that this book will encourage you to keep all the puzzle pieces on the table. Every passage in the New Testament is too valuable to distort in order to make it fit a pre-conceived system. Eternal destinies are at stake!

I have also sought to show how both warnings and assurance and faith and works can be brought together. This is, of course, a massive undertaking and in this short book I have only been able to point in what I think is the right direction.

In regard to the warning passages, I have argued that they are directed at genuine Christians and are not just hypothetical. The danger is real for those who fail to faithfully persevere. Thanks to the assurance passages, the reality of this danger does not leave us paralyzed in fear—God is willing, able, and active in our salvation. He has accomplished everything necessary for salvation, and has provided us with every resource needed for the journey. God is committed to finishing the work he began in us! In this process God uses the very real warnings to motivate us to flee sinful choices, habits, and addictions and pursue righteousness. The warnings make it crystal clear that we are in danger if we willingly choose to walk away from God's promises and protection. If I willfully abandon Christ I ought to be afraid.

According to the New Testament, our assurance of final salvation is not linked exclusively to a past experience of salvation but also includes our present experience of salvation. We have confidence that we will be saved in the future, not just because we have memories of a conversion/salvation experience in the past, but because we are also joyfully experiencing God's salvation in the present. Assurance of future salvation is primarily based upon our experience of salvation in the present, that is, our perseverance: "faith working through love" (Galatians 5:6). A living faith in the present provides far more assurance that a dead faith from the past.

Both warnings and assurances are included in the New Testament because we have different needs at different points in our Christian lives. Sometimes we desperately need to hear the warnings so that godly fear will keep us on the right path, while other times we desperately need to hear God's assurances of our salvation to prevent us from falling over the cliff into a pit of hopelessness and despair. Both are needed and neither should be minimized.

I have also suggested that perseverance should be understood as perseverance in faith and works. Faith and works are inseparably connected in a holistic human response to God's saving initiative. Perseverance is simply the continuation of this saving holistic response until the end of our lives. We are saved by genuine faith, and whoever ceases to believe will not be saved. Genuine faith is holistic; it includes works and impacts every aspect of our being: our thoughts, beliefs, words, and actions.

There is no such thing as a compartmentalized person who can genuinely believe something as powerful and life transforming as the Gospel without also being affected in every aspect of life. It is fine, of course, to think that faith must precede works since we think about things before we act but genuine saving faith cannot exist in isolation from one's actions. Any supposed faith that doesn't impact our actions falls short of saving faith. Our actions reveal what we really believe, not just what we say we believe or might pretend to believe. Our true and deepest beliefs are always evident by our decisions.

THE HOLY SPIRIT

We have discussed at length the connection of salvation to genuine faith at every step along the way from initial conversion to final salvation. Perseverance is the working out of the salvation which begins with conversion and leads to final salvation. This experiencing of salvation in the present through perseverance is entirely dependent upon God's power and ability to save us and our continuing response to God in genuine and holistic faith. As Peter notes, we are being guarded in the present (1) *by God's power* (2) *through faith* until we might receive our final inheritance (1 Peter 1:5).

There is still one major thing missing from our discussion, the secret ingredient, the ingredient that transforms a simple recipe into a culinary mastery, the ingredient which changes everything. This is the great game-changer of the Christian life. In chapter one above, we looked at how Jesus' life, death, and resurrection broke through the wall of time separating our present from God's future. Because of this momentous and history-altering event, all sorts of things associated with God's future salvation in the new heavens and new earth have flooded into the present evil and broken world.

The Holy Spirit is chief among the end-time realities that followed Jesus' resurrection through the wall of time separating God's future new creation from our present broken world. Because of Jesus' resurrection and enthronement at God's right hand, the Holy Spirit has been unleashed in this present world to dwell within believers (John 7:38–39; 14:17), guide us into truth (John 16:13), provide access to God (Ephesians 2:18), equip us with spiritual gifts (1 Corinthians 12:4–7), produce the fruit of new creation within us (Galatians 5:22–23), provide assurance of our adoption by God (Romans 8:15–16; Galatians 4:6) and of our future salvation (2 Corinthians 1:22; 5:5; Ephesians 1:13–14; 4:30). The fruit of the Spirit is thus the fruit of the life of our future existence in God's kingdom being supernaturally produced and developed in the midst of this present evil age (Galatians 5:22–23).

The Holy Spirit provides the power and driving force behind everything we have been discussing in this book: faith, works, salvation, and perseverance. The third person of the Trinity is actively at work in the present to lead us to saving faith and regeneration (Titus 3:5), and sustain us in this saving faith until the end of our lives. This is the final response to the charge that the necessity of perseverance for final salvation is some kind of legalistic works righteousness. The Spirit is the power behind our salvation throughout the entire process from initial conversion to final glorification. There is no room for merit or boasting and we can do nothing with our petty human power to add to his power. As Zechariah aptly wrote, "Not by might, nor by power, but by my Spirit, says the Lord of hosts" (Zechariah 4:6).

Our human response of holistic faith is energized and maintained by the grace of God and the activity of the Spirit in our lives. Our perseverance and final salvation will never depend upon grit and determination but desperate surrender to, and trust in, the one who is able to keep us from falling. May God richly strengthen you with his power and Spirit as you persevere in this journey of life to your final destination in his eternal kingdom!

QUESTIONS FOR PERSONAL REFLECTION OR SMALL-GROUP DISCUSSION

1. How would you describe the effects and activity of the Holy Spirit in your own personal life? This could be in terms of big and sudden transformations or in subtle and small day-by-day changes.

2. How has this study of perseverance and salvation in the New Testament changed or impacted you? The New Testament was not written to simply provide information to the intellectually curious but to transform its hearers.

Appendix

Pliny the Younger

Governor of Pontus/Bithynia from 111–113 AD

Pliny, *Letters* 10.96–97 (Radice, LCL)

Pliny to the Emperor Trajan

It is my custom to refer all my difficulties to you, Sir, for no one is better able to resolve my doubts and to inform my ignorance.

I have never been present at an examination of Christians. Consequently, I do not know the nature or the extent of the punishments usually meted out to them, nor the grounds for starting an investigation and how far it should be pressed. Nor am I at all sure whether any distinction should be made between them on the grounds of age, or if young people and adults should be treated alike; whether a pardon ought to be granted to anyone retracting his beliefs, or if he has once professed Christianity, he shall gain nothing by renouncing it; and whether it is the mere name of Christian which is punishable, even if innocent of crime, or rather the crimes associated with the name.

For the moment this is the line I have taken with all persons brought before me on the charge of being Christians. I have asked them in person if they are Christians, and if they admit it, I repeat the question a second and third time, with a warning of the punishment awaiting them. If they persist, I order them to be led away for execution; for, whatever the nature of their admission, I am convinced that their stubbornness and unshakeable obstinacy ought not to go unpunished. There have been others similarly fanatical who are Roman citizens. I have entered them on the list of persons to be sent to Rome for trial.

Now that I have begun to deal with this problem, as so often happens, the charges are becoming more widespread and increasing in variety. An anonymous pamphlet has been circulated which contains the names of a number of accused persons. Among these I considered that I should dismiss any who denied that they were or ever had been Christians when they had repeated after me a formula of invocation to the gods and had made offerings of wine and incense to your statue (which I had ordered to be brought into court for this purpose along with the images of the gods), and furthermore had reviled the name of Christ: none of which things, I understand, any genuine Christian can be induced to do.

Others, whose names were given to me by an informer, first admitted the charge and then denied it; they said that they had ceased to be Christians two or more years previously, and some of them even twenty years ago. They all did reverence to your statue and the images of the gods in the same way as the others, and reviled the name of Christ. They also declared that the sum total of their guilt or error amounted to no more than this: they had met regularly before dawn on a fixed day to chant verses alternately among themselves in honour of Christ as if to a god, and also to bind themselves by oath, not for any criminal purpose, but to abstain from theft, robbery and adultery, to commit no breach of trust and not to deny a deposit when called upon to restore it. After this ceremony it had been their custom to disperse and reassemble later to take food of an ordinary, harmless kind; but they had in fact given up this practice since my edict, issued on your instructions, which banned all political societies. This made me decide it was all the more necessary to extract the truth by torture from two slave-women, whom they call deaconesses. I found nothing but a degenerate sort of cult carried to extravagant lengths.

I have therefore postponed any further examination and hastened to consult you. The question seems to me to be worthy of your consideration, especially in view of the number of persons endangered; for a great many individuals of every age and class, both men and women, are being brought to trial, and this is likely to continue. It is not only the towns, but villages and rural districts too which are infected through contact with this wretched cult. I think though that it is still possible for it to be checked and directed to better ends, for there is no doubt that people have begun to throng the temples which had been almost entirely deserted for a long time; the sacred rites which had been allowed to lapse are being performed again, and flesh of sacrificial victims is on sale everywhere, though up till recently scarcely anyone could be found to buy it. It is easy to infer from this that a great many people could be reformed if they were given an opportunity to repent.

Trajan to Pliny

You have followed the right course of procedure, my dear Pliny, in your examination of the cases of persons charged with being Christians, for it is impossible to lay down a general rule to a fixed formula. These people must not be hunted out; if they are brought before you and the charge against them is proved, they must be punished, but in the case of anyone who denies that he is a Christian, and makes it clear that he is not by offering prayers to our gods, he is to be pardoned as a result of his repentance however suspect his past conduct may be. But pamphlets circulated anonymously must play no part in any accusation. They create the worst sort of precedent and are quite out of keeping with the spirit of our age.

Recommended Reading

This book has intentionally avoided interacting with other authors in order to provide a short accessible introduction focused completely on the biblical texts. For those interested, I have interacted with the relevant scholarship on these topics in much greater depth in the following publications.

Stewart, Alexander. "Cosmology, Eschatology, and Soteriology in Hebrews: A Synthetic Analysis." *Bulletin for Biblical Research* 20 (2010): 545–560.

———. "James, Soteriology, and Synergism." *Tyndale Bulletin* 61 (2010): 293–310.

———. "When are Christians Saved and Why Does it Matter? An Investigation into the Rhetorical Force of First Peter's Inaugurated Soteriology." *Trinity Journal* 32 (2011): 221–235.

———. *Soteriology as Motivation in the Apocalypse of John.* Gorgias Biblical Studies 61. Piscataway, N.J.: Gorgias Press, 2015.

For those interested in other perspectives and more detailed discussions of particular texts I would recommend the following books. You may not agree with all the authors but they each value God's Word and are seeking to keep all the puzzle pieces on the table.

Bates, Matthew W. *Salvation by Allegiance Alone: Rethinking Faith, Works, and the Gospel of Jesus the King.* Grand Rapids, Mich.: Baker Academic, 2017.

Marshall, I. Howard. *Kept by the Power of God: A Study of Perseverance and Falling Away.* Minneapolis, Minn.: Bethany Fellowship, 1969.

Schreiner, Thomas, and Ardel Caneday. *The Race Set Before Us: A Biblical Theology of Perseverance & Assurance.* Downers Grove, Ill.: InterVarsity, 2001.

Stanley, Alan P. *Salvation Is More Complicated Than You Think: A Study on the Teachings of Jesus.* Colorado Springs, Colo.: Paternoster, 2007.

Stanley, Alan P. ed. *Four Views on the Role of Works at the Final Judgment.* Counterpoints: Bible and Theology. Grand Rapids, Mich.: Zondervan, 2013.

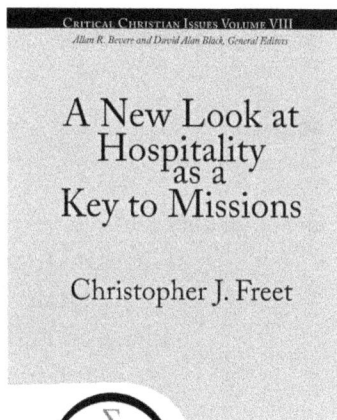

MORE FROM ENERGION PUBLICATIONS

Personal Study
Holy Smoke! Unholy Fire	Bob McKibben	$14.99
The Jesus Paradigm	David Alan Black	$17.99
When People Speak for God	Henry Neufeld	$17.99
The Sacred Journey	Chris Surber	$11.99

Christian Living
Faith in the Public Square	Robert D. Cornwall	$16.99
Grief: Finding the Candle of Light	Jody Neufeld	$8.99
Crossing the Street	Robert LaRochelle	$16.99
Life in the Spirit	J. Hamilton Weston	$12.99

Bible Study
Learning and Living Scripture	Lentz/Neufeld	$12.99
Inspiration: Hard Questions, Honest Answers	Alden Thompson	$29.99
Colossians & Philemon	Allan R. Bevere	$12.99
Ephesians: A Participatory Study Guide	Robert D. Cornwall	$9.99

Theology
Christian Archy	David Alan Black	$9.99
The Politics of Witness	Allan R. Bevere	$9.99
Ultimate Allegiance	Robert D. Cornwall	$9.99
From Here to Eternity	Bruce Epperly	$5.99
The Journey to the Undiscovered Country	William Powell Tuck	$9.99
Eschatology: A Participatory Study Guide	Edward W. H. Vick	$9.99
The Adventist's Dilemma	Edward W. H. Vick	$14.99

Ministry
Clergy Table Talk	Kent Ira Groff	$9.99
Thrive	Ruth Fletcher	$14.99
Out of the Office: A Theology of Ministry	Bob Cornwall	$9.99

Generous Quantity Discounts Available
Dealer Inquiries Welcome
Energion Publications — P.O. Box 841
Gonzalez, FL_ 32560
Website: http://energionpubs.com
Phone: (850) 525-3916

www.ingramcontent.com/pod-product-compliance
Lightning Source LLC
Chambersburg PA
CBHW051844040426
42447CB00006B/694